Benjamin Crismon

40 DAYS

A Lenten Journey Through Exodus

Nashville

40 Days

A Lenten Journey Through Exodus

Library of Congress Control Number: 2025946720
978-1-7910-4101-4

MANUFACTURED IN THE UNITED STATES OF AMERICA

Contents

Introduction

The season of Lent is the period of time between Ash Wednesday and Easter. Its forty days, excluding Sundays, are a time of fasting, waiting, and spiritual discipline, with the hope and goal of deepening our faith and fully experiencing the power of Christ's victory over death on Easter Sunday.

My experience with Christianity has always been within the membership of a church that follows the liturgical calendar. This calendar includes the seasons of the Church Year, beginning in Advent with preparation for the birth of Christ; there are seasons celebrating Pentecost, Epiphany, Easter, and even those that recognize the periods of time in which nothing "special" is going on, other than the usual passage of time as a part of God's wondrous creation. We call this Ordinary Time. But far from ordinary it is.

Growing up as a United Methodist, I was always very familiar with these natural flows and rhythms. But it wasn't just Methodism that shaped me in this way; I went to a Lutheran grade school and a Catholic high school that followed the same calendar. I grew up with nearly all my friends living in a world with both a secular calendar and a church calendar, where days like Maundy Thursday and Ash Wednesday were just as normal as President's Day and Labor Day. It wasn't until I began full-time ministry that I really understood how many faithful Christians there were who didn't follow these traditions. When I would talk about "giving something up for Lent" or coming to an Ash Wednesday service, I sensed that these things did not have the same emotional resonance for others as they did for me. This led me to deeper study the origins of these seasons, particularly the season of Lent. Where does it come from? Why do we observe it? Why is it forty days? And why do we observe it the way we do?

Forty is an important number in Scripture. It recalls a time in the history of our faith when our ancestors experienced forty years of hunger, suffering, and spiritual discipline with the hope and goal of living into God's covenant for their future as the Israelites wandered in the wilderness after being freed by God from their slavery in Egypt. Forty is also the number of days that Jesus fasted in the wilderness, the amount of time Noah and family spent upon the Ark, the number of days Elijah hid in the wilderness after his defeat of the prophets of Baal. One hundred and forty-six times the number forty is mentioned in Scripture, and in almost every instance it means a period of testing, struggle, or preparation.

There is a powerful connection between our Lenten experience and the book of Exodus. And most of it revolves around a number: forty. Forty days of Lent, forty years in the wilderness, forty chapters in the Book of Exodus.

Throughout this devotional, we will be walking through one chapter of the Book of Exodus each day. Taking a few minutes to read the chapter on your own before coming to this book will allow you to make the most of this season. The Book of Exodus will be a launching point for us to connect with God's enduring fidelity and deep love as well as both our ancestors' faithfulness and spiritual failures. Through it all, we open our hearts for God to use this story to shape our story as we seek to become more faithful disciples of Jesus.

These are your forty days—a time to take seriously what it means to wrestle with your faithfulness, dive into your relationship with God, and to prepare yourself for the glory that awaits on the other end of this time. Forty days to listen to God's leadership, hear God's promises, and deepen your faith. Forty days to struggle, fast, and hunger to grow in your dependence on God's provision. Forty days to prepare your heart and soul to have the most meaningful Easter that you have ever experienced in your life. These are your forty days to allow God to transform your heart. Embrace the journey and the difficulty that may come, for these are nothing compared to the Promised Land that awaits us on the other side.

DAY 1

Exodus 1

Key Verse: Exodus 1:8

To fully understand the Exodus story, we have to remember God's covenant promise to Abraham, Isaac, Jacob, and Joseph—a promise that this family would grow so large it would outnumber the stars, that it would dwell in a wonderful land, and that it would have the presence of God with it always. Through this the family members would be blessed to be a blessing. The future of the people was bright, for they were God's people.

However, that bright future was tarnished because of a drought throughout the land. Needing food and assistance, God provided for them through their patriarch, Joseph. God led Joseph to a position of power, and he protected and provided for his tribal family.

But time went by, a generation passed, and another threat to God's promise suddenly arose; one we see in our key verse for today: a new pharaoh who feels no obligations or loyalties to this foreign people living in his land, a people he begins to see as a threat to his rule.

We may have experienced something like this when a supervisor we love deeply retires and is replaced by someone we don't have a relationship with and maybe don't trust. Overnight, all our hard work and respect has to be rebuilt from the ground up. The Israelites certainly must have felt this stress and anxiety, and that feeling began to change their relationship with God. God has promised them a land of their own, but they have been living in Egypt for generations. To make matters worse, they have been enslaved by this new pharaoh. The other part of God's promise, to become a mighty and numerous nation, is in jeopardy as well. We can imagine why their faith might be shaken.

At the beginning of this Lenten journey, we have to acknowledge that we are not all starting from the best place in our relationship with God. Often, we find ourselves in the place of our ancestors, feeling as though God's promises in our lives are being threatened. These promises are endangered either by outside forces of evil or our own sinful choices. We are stressed, anxious, depressed, and overwhelmed. We want to be more faithful and more loving, but we are tired and cannot seem to feel God's presence or leadership. It leads us to wonder where God is in the midst of our difficulties. Even from the outset of our journey, the odds are stacked against us.

But let us find comfort in the truth. God is working on our behalf, just as God was in the lives of the Israelites so many years ago. Begin this season in the sure truth that God is providing a way for you, fighting beside you, and protecting you from behind. God is lovingly preparing a place for you to find life abundant and life eternal. This is the first day of a journey that will lead us through the wilderness, to the cross, and finally to the empty tomb, with Christ victorious. Let us cling to the truth we find in the Psalms. As Psalm 46:1 says, "God is our refuge and strength, a very present help in trouble." Let us start our forty days in the refuge of God's love.

- Have you ever felt like something was preventing you from experiencing God's presence? Was it internal or external?
- How can a lack of knowledge, like the new pharaoh's lack of knowledge about Joseph, lead us into trouble in our lives of faith?

DAY 2

Exodus 2

Key Verse: Exodus 2:6

Today we are introduced to Moses, the figure who will join us throughout the rest of our Lenten journey. Before he was even born, his life was at stake. The threat against God's people was palpable, as the new pharaoh had ordered the genocide of all male children born to the Israelites. Moses's mother went to great lengths to save her child and hid him in the river, where he was found by Pharaoh's daughter. It is here that we see a powerful emotion come over this nameless princess: pity.

"Pity" (*chamal*) is a strong word in Hebrew that also can mean "to spare." In saving the child, she enters into an alliance with him and is prepared to be his protector. She knows that this child is a Hebrew baby and that she is risking the life of the child, and her own, if she brings him into her care. This is more than feeling sorry for the baby; this is an act of ultimate compassion and mercy.

We often view pity as something to avoid, hoping that we are strong enough to never need someone else's pity. The word *pitiful* also has another connotation: It can be used to describe something that is deserving of our sympathy but also something deserving of contempt (as in "he was given a pitiful wage for his labor"). Clearly, this is not how we are meant to see Moses, a baby completely incapable of helping himself. The princess's pity was life saving for him.

This reminds me of the story of Dave Borgal, a successful sports journalist early in his career who felt a calling to go into education. The only job he could find was as a guidance counselor, which wasn't in his specialty, but he needed a place to land. In this role, he found that many students in low-income schools found the college application process difficult and daunting and would often not apply at all due to these obstacles. He took a deep interest in their lives and fought alongside them to help them apply to the right schools and obtain scholarships and financial aid. He began to see that this wasn't just an issue at his school but was much larger. This led Dave to launch a nonprofit called Bottom Line that would help students apply to and successfully stay in college. From their humble beginnings in 1997, today Bottom Line is in five major metro areas, and thousands of students each year receive the help they need to continue and successfully complete their educations. Dave Borgal saw the struggles of those in need. These struggles pained him, too, and this spurred him into life-changing action.

There is so much to learn here. In the face of the enemy, we find comfort. In a time of death, life is secured. When all seems lost, a glimmer of hope appears. This can happen through pity, when another person or our God sees our struggle and comes to our aid.

This raises a powerful question for us: When have we experienced this same compassion and mercy from God, and when have we offered it to those around us? Let us be a people who accept the compassion of God, who longs to rescue and redeem us, and share that same love with others.

- Have you ever felt like you didn't deserve God's pity (compassion and mercy)? What made you feel that way? Do you feel that God's love is always present, regardless of your past mistakes?
- Who in your life do you need to pity or have greater sympathy for? Is there someone who needs an extra dose of compassion and mercy? How can you offer that to them this week?

DAY 3

Exodus 3

Key Verse: Exodus 3:4-5

I will never forget the first time my daughter used my first name to address me in public. There is something so powerful the first time you hear your precious little girl say "Ben, Ben!!" instead of lovingly calling "Daddy." I was immediately shocked and startled into the seriousness of the situation. It was the fall of 2022, and she had just turned nine. We had decided to take a quick trip to St. Louis to see the Gateway Arch, head to Grant's Farm, and as the highlight, take in our family's first professional baseball game.

We made our way to Busch Stadium, and the crowds were thick on this warm September evening. After finding our seats, the kids wanted to get some ballpark snacks, and so the four of us trekked off in search of nachos, cotton candy, and hot dogs. My daughter, the oldest of our three kids, was at the end of the hand-holding chain, with her two brothers between us. We were weaving through the crowd, trying to stay together, but it was loud and chaotic. In the midst of moving through the madness, she got separated and was struggling to keep up. I couldn't hear her shouting, "Daddy!" over the roar of the crowd and the music, so she resorted to more drastic measures: She said my name.

I stopped in my tracks, hearing the sweet voice of my little girl, shouting my name with fear forming a lump in her throat. Immediately, I turned around and reconnected with her, assuring her that we would go slower and everything would be just fine. We got the snacks, enjoyed the game, and while I am sure that this is an event she no longer remembers, it is one I will never forget. There is something powerful about being called by name.

Moses understood this very well. We need to put ourselves in Moses's sandals for a minute. After killing an Egyptian in defense of a Hebrew man, giving up his position in the royal household, and fleeing Egypt for his life, he is terrified. He finds safety and eventually a family among a nomadic people, hoping that his past stays in the past. He tries desperately to move on from both his Hebrew and Egyptian identities, marrying a Midianite. But God has more in store for Moses.

While Moses is tending sheep, he hears his name being called. Hearing someone say his name could have meant a threat, perhaps a soldier sent from the pharaoh to arrest Moses. It could have been anyone from his former life coming to disrupt the peace he had found. The idea must have sent shivers down his spine. After hearing my daughter that day at the baseball game, I can imagine the feeling.

But the one shouting Moses's name is God, and God is summoning Moses to become a part of God's great work to save God's people from slavery and death. God has a calling for Moses, a vocation to live out.

The same is true for you. Sometimes, though, like Moses, this voice of God calling out can frighten us, as God might be calling us to leave our old lives of sin and shame behind. It might give us pause because God might have a calling that is beyond our comfort zone. Nonetheless, I want you to pause a moment today and listen for God to say your name. God knows you, loves you, and offers you forgiveness and salvation. Even more, God invites you to participate in the great work of building God's kingdom, to be a part of the salvation of all humanity. But the voice of God may not be as loud or as bold as a burning bush, so be ready to pay attention and listen well.

- Have you ever heard someone say your name and it stopped you in your tracks? How did that make you feel? Can you imagine how Moses must have felt?
- Have you ever heard God's calling in your life? What did God say to you? Do you need to hear from God again?

DAY 4

Exodus 4

Key Verses: 4:1-5

The calling Moses received is a daunting one: a commission to go back to Egypt and demand that the most powerful man in all the world, Pharaoh, should let his enslaved labor force free. Add on to that the fact that Moses was a wanted criminal who would be facing punishment for the murder of the Egyptian taskmaster. There was a reason he was out in the wilderness, and it was to stay far, far away from Egypt.

But maybe one of the most difficult obstacles was the fact that Moses had no real relationship with God's people. He had not been raised with them, he had no lifelong friends in that community, and we don't really know the extent of the relationship he had with his siblings or other family. Can you imagine being told that you were going to lead a group of people you scarcely knew and who probably didn't want you as their leader?

The closest thing I have ever experienced to this is my work as an itinerant pastor in the United Methodist Church. While the churches I have served always welcomed me warmly and were ready to receive my leadership, there were moments early in my vocation when I would hear things like this: "You're young enough to be my grandchild" or "My kids are older than you." What I heard them saying was, "You are far too young to be doing this job." Over time, each congregation came to value my leadership, but I had to work with God to prove myself worthy of their respect. As I get older, I am sure there will be a time when I wish that people would make comments about how young I look, but I digress. With all these obstacles stacked against Moses, you can imagine his anxiety and fear and understand his apparent reluctance to accept and fully commit to God's calling.

Moses relays each and every one of these fears to God, trying to convince God that he is not the man for the job. But for every one of Moses's objections, God has a response. For every protestation, God has a solution. These signs from God are not just meant to quell his fears but also to become a signpost to all the people, including the Egyptians, of God's power and might. God wanted everyone to know that he intended to save his people from their horrible conditions.

John Wesley, the founder of the Methodist movement, believed that all of Jesus's disciples were called into some kind of ministry or vocation. That didn't mean they were called to ordained ministry but that God wanted to use them to build God's kingdom in some way.

I believe that but add that there is a calling for each station of our lives. We aren't just called as young people or as parents or as retired people. God has work for us to do in each of those periods of our lives. These callings may be different as we gain new skills, add life experiences, and live in new places, so we must be ready to hear God's call. But as we start to listen to God's voice calling us into some new level of devotion, a new ministry or program, or a fresh start in life, are we meeting that calling with our own fears and anxieties? Are you coming up with a laundry list of reasons why you cannot accomplish God's calling? Are you feeling like Moses?

These feelings are reasonable, and we shouldn't try to suppress or deny them. God didn't get angry with Moses for protesting, so be open and honest with God. Ask yourself: What responses and solutions do I need to hear from God? How can I learn to trust God to guide me where God calls me to? These questions will be with us throughout this journey. Let's keep walking.

- Have you ever felt God guiding you to do something? How did that feel?
- Were you able to overcome the fear and anxiety, particularly if it was a new thing?
- How did you feel God's presence as you followed God's guidance?

DAY 5

Exodus 5

Key Verses: Exodus 5:18-23

Pharaoh, upon hearing Moses and Aaron detail God's demands, dismisses them and the God they represent. Pharaoh considers himself divine and so do his people. The story is setting up an epic battle between the God of the Hebrews and the king who thinks he is a god. It is no surprise, then, that Pharaoh refuses to acknowledge that Moses and his God are worthy of his attention. As a result, Pharaoh turns to practical matters: He cannot lose his labor force.

We know that slavery was a vital resource for the Egyptians, used to help this mighty kingdom with their farming and building projects. Losing a major portion of these slaves would threaten Egyptian economic potential and prospects. Pharaoh cannot let that happen by any means. He cannot be seen as weak or ineffectual, so direct action is needed.

Seeking to squelch a rebellion, Pharaoh intensifies the workload of the Hebrew slaves. In turn, upon finding out who was responsible for this sudden increase, the leaders of the

Hebrews blame Moses and Aaron. Their feelings aren't misplaced, but they are ignorant of God's broader plans. You can imagine their feelings: Out of nowhere Moses, who grew up in the Egyptian palace but is a Hebrew, shows up to set them free after being gone for years. And in his first attempt, he makes their lives significantly worse. This seems to be going nowhere fast, and Moses feels the pressure.

So, he quickly starts throwing the blame back at God. Moses didn't really want to do this to begin with and wasn't convinced it would work. Now, he has been rejected by Pharaoh and the Hebrews. He is angry and disappointed in God, and he lets God know it. In fact, Moses accuses God of doing nothing at all: "Since I first came to Pharaoh to speak in your name, he has mistreated this people, and you have done nothing at all to deliver your people" (verse 23).

I have said things like this, and I bet you have as well. When things don't go our way and we don't get the answer we want, we are quick to accuse—accusing God of picking on us or even completely abandoning us.

I remember visiting with a woman struggling with Parkinson's. She was tired and hurting, with little hope of returning to her previous life. I asked if she was angry with God, and she said that she wasn't, but she was deeply disappointed in God because she didn't feel like God was doing anything at all to help her. She just couldn't feel God's presence or strength and was heartbroken over that.

I felt this way when my wife and I were struggling through a season of infertility. We were young and healthy people; we had been married for five years and were in a perfect place to start our family. Both of us wanted to have children and were watching all our friends get pregnant, and all we could do was keep waiting for it to happen for us. So, we waited and waited. Nothing. With each passing month, hope started getting harder and harder to find, and the feelings of rejection began to surface. Baby shower invitations became things of great pain as we longed to celebrate a pregnancy of our own. Eventually, I remember running to God in the way Moses did, full of anger and frustration. I remember telling God, "You gave me a calling to be a husband and a father, and you did the same for Mary. Why would you call us to this and not give us the opportunity to do it?" I was angry, hurt, and scared.

The good news is that God listened to an angry Moses in the same way that God listened to a scared Moses. God listened to me as well, and God will listen to you. Do not hide your anger or frustration from God; let God know about it, open up, and prepare yourself for God's response. Tomorrow, we will see what God had to say to Moses.

- When in your life have you felt like God abandoned you?
- How long did you feel that way? How did you regain trust? If you still feel that way, tell God and listen for God's response.

DAY 6

Exodus 6

Key Verses: Exodus 6:6-9

This is one of the most important, realistic, and heartbreaking moments in all of Exodus. In our key verses, we see God's response to the people who feel abandoned and alone. God declares that these are his own people and that he will act as their redeemer, setting them free and moving them into a new land. God is powerfully affirming the desire to keep promises to his people. This announcement is one of the most beautiful statements of God's character we find in Scripture.

And then we are hit with the twist in the plot. We expect that Moses and the people, upon hearing these promises, would be filled with joy and hope, throwing their hands into the sky in celebration. That's what we would expect upon hearing such grand good news. But that isn't what happens. Their spirits were broken by the cruelty they had experienced. The words of God were not enough to bring the hope they so desperately needed.

Years ago, a man stopped by my office and sat down in the chair across my desk. He was a strong and vibrant man, husband to a beautiful wife and father to two young children. He was a successful banker and seemed to have everything. But inside he was more like the Hebrew slaves. He was broken by the weight of guilt and shame. As soon as he sat down, he looked at me with tears in his eyes, before completely coming undone. With tears streaming down his face, he began to share with me what he had done. An affair at work led to his termination and threatened his marriage and family. His world was absolutely falling apart, and there was no one to blame but himself.

As we talked about forgiveness and restoration, about God's unconditional love and fresh starts, I could tell that he didn't believe a word I was saying. I realized over the course of our conversation that although this man had been coming to church for years, he didn't really believe in Jesus; he hadn't fully accepted the gospel in his heart and mind. So, in this moment of deep pain and heartbreak, he wasn't able to believe those words about God's love because he had never experienced it. His response to God's promise was just like that of the Hebrews in Exodus.

Maybe you have experienced something like this as well. Perhaps in moments of heartbreak and pain, feeling abandoned and alone, you couldn't bring yourself to trust God's presence and promise. The words alone weren't enough for you to believe God was really there or God was capable of making things better in your life. There is something so visceral and powerful about this part of the story, something real that we all experience.

But there is also some great news here. God doesn't get angry with the people for feeling this way. God doesn't condemn their lack of faith or unwillingness to follow Moses. Instead, God leans in even more, willing to go to whatever lengths necessary to redeem and save the people. Read that again: God does whatever it takes. The same is true for you. Wherever you are on this journey, know that there is no mountain too tall or valley too deep for God's love to claim and find you. God wasn't done with the Hebrews, and God isn't done with you.

- How do you respond to the surprising reaction of the Israelites? Does their lack of faith make you frustrated? Do you find their reaction unfortunate but understandable?
- How can you more clearly hear God speaking to you as He did to the Israelites? What spiritual practice might make you more able to listen to God?

DAY 7

Exodus 7

Key Verses: Exodus 7:16

There are a variety of wake-up calls we receive. Growing up, the first kind of wake-up calls I remember were from my golden retriever, Pumpkin. Each morning, my mother sent her into my room and told her to get me up. She gently nudged my face with her cold nose, and I knew it was time to get moving.

As I grew older, after Pumpkin died, the wakeups were still kind, but less gentle, as my mom hollered up the stairs and told me it was time to "rise and shine." Then came college and the seventeen alarms I had to set for my 8:00 a.m. Philosophy 101 class. I don't miss those mornings one bit. After that came the sweet and gentle words of my wife, wishing me a great day. Those were swiftly replaced by the knees and elbows of our precious kids far too early on Saturday mornings. Now, I have reached the age where I don't need a wake-up call other than my own circadian rhythm. From soft and gentle to loud and blaring, wake-up calls come in lots of forms and flavors.

God often sends wake-up calls into our lives. Some are like the college alarm clock and come in undeniable ways, grabbing our attention and ensuring that we understand what it is God wants us to know. We have seen this already in our journey through Exodus, when God speaks to Moses through the burning bush. But there are other times that God is far more subtle, more nuanced in his communication with us. In these moments, if we aren't really paying attention, we can miss what God is trying to relate to us. These whispers of the Holy Spirit often carry helpful guidance and meaningful reminders of God's presence and love.

Sometimes, though, what wakes us up isn't a planned alarm but rather some noise in the night that demands our attention. Hearing the storm sirens blaring or an alert on our phones can jar us into action. In the same way, the calls from God can also carry warnings to turn away from sinfulness and harmful behaviors.

We see God offer one of these wake-up calls to Pharaoh in our key verse for today. In fact, it is found in just two words: "until now." Until now, Pharaoh hasn't listened to God, hasn't believed that God is worthy of being feared or respected. "Until now"—two words that carry so much meaning. First, they imply that Pharaoh is expected to listen. They also imply something like: *You haven't yet listened, but you will soon.* This is a boldly confident speech from Yahweh. God is going to bend the ear of the most powerful man in the world, and soon.

The God who wields this power stands in your corner. The God who is greater than any evil or challenge loves you and wants to provide for you. The God who reigns wants to know you and be known by you. The truth is that God wants to communicate with you, to share messages of love as well as call out sinfulness. So, let's listen more closely to hear the whispers God has for us.

- Do you often find yourself distracted? How can you be more present in your day-to-day life so that you can hear the whispers of God?
- Are you more distracted by your internal monologue or external noise? Often the voice in our heads is louder than any noise. How can you work to still your mind and quiet your soul to listen to God?

DAY 8

Exodus 8

Key Verses: Exodus 8:10-15

We find ourselves today in the heart of the plague narrative of Exodus, where God unleashes a series of curses upon Egypt in a powerful display to set the Israelites free. Up to this point, Pharaoh has been both unimpressed and unmoved by any of God's actions against him. His heart is hardened, his ego inflated, and his grip on power unwavering. Yet God, in the relentless pursuit of justice and liberation, continues to press in. This time, God uses a plague of frogs to try and break through.

Can you imagine what it would be like to wake to frogs all over your house? Not just a few here and there, but frogs *everywhere*: in your bed, in your food, underfoot with every step, their constant croaking echoing through the walls. It's a scene of absolute chaos and turmoil. It's easy to read past the details of this plague, but when you pause to picture it, the terror becomes palpable. The very thing Pharaoh once controlled—his kingdom, his palace, his comfort—is now overrun by something as seemingly small and insignificant as frogs.

What's remarkable about this moment isn't just the physical nuisance of the frogs but how Pharaoh responds. For the first time, the most powerful man in the world is forced to admit there is something he cannot fix. He can't make the frogs disappear. He can't command them away. All of his wealth, power, and influence are useless in the face of this invasion. Pharaoh is brought to the humbling realization that there is something outside of his control, and he has to ask for help.

Pharaoh calls on Moses, asking him to pray to God to take the frogs away. It's a crack in the armor of his ego, however small. Moses agrees, but not without making it clear what is really at stake. This moment isn't just about removing frogs—it's about God's power. The entire narrative of the plagues is a battle not between Moses and Pharaoh but between Pharaoh's illusion of control and God's undeniable sovereignty.

Pharaoh's response stands as a warning to us all. How often do we resist acknowledging God's power until life forces us to? We cling to the illusion that we are in control, managing our schedules, building our careers, keeping our families running, until something happens that reminds us how fragile our sense of control really is. It's easy to look at Pharaoh's arrogance and think, *I would never be like that.* But pride has a way of creeping into our hearts quietly, making us believe that we can handle things on our own.

Maybe you've experienced a moment like Pharaoh's, when life threw something at you that you simply couldn't fix. A health crisis, a broken relationship, a financial struggle. Those moments, painful as they are, can become invitations to recognize God's power. They remind us that we were never meant to carry the weight of control alone. God's sovereignty isn't a threat, it's a gift. When we surrender to God's power, we discover the deep relief that comes with letting go.

But what if we didn't wait for the frogs to pile up before turning to God? What if we practiced humility and surrender every day, before the chaos set in? Scripture teaches us that humility is not something that happens to us—it's something we choose. It's the daily decision to acknowledge that God is God and we are not. It's the practice of prayerfully handing over our plans, our worries, and our need for control.

My prayer for you is that you would recognize God's sovereignty not in the way Pharaoh did—through resistance and hardship—but through a heart that is open and obedient. May we be a people who lay down our pride, who invite God into every corner of our lives, and who trust that God is with us.

- When was a time you became keenly aware of God's power in your life? Was it in a moment of crisis or in the quiet, ordinary rhythms of life?
- How can you practice humility today—not out of fear or resignation, but out of trust in a God who is always working for your good?

DAY 9

Exodus 9

Key Verses: Exodus 9:16

Let's be honest, reading the stories of these plagues can be difficult. It makes us uncomfortable to witness God send plague after plague upon the people of Egypt. These passages challenge us, forcing us to wrestle with the parts of God's character that feel harsh or confusing. But this struggle is exactly why they are so important on our Lenten journey. If we are going to pledge our lives in obedience and service to God, we need to examine and embrace the parts of God we don't fully understand. Lent isn't just about reflection and repentance; it's about deepening our relationship with God, even when that relationship stretches us.

The plague narrative is more than just a series of dramatic punishments. It's a power struggle between God and the Egyptian empire. Egypt was a dominant power during this period, with Pharaoh claiming to be a living deity. The message was clear: Pharaoh was in control, and no one, certainly not the god of an enslaved people, could challenge his authority. But God steps into this story to reveal this as an illusion.

Each plague is a strategic blow, not just against the Egyptians, but also against the very gods they worshipped. The Nile, their source of life, turns to blood. Frogs, gnats, and flies swarm the land. Livestock perishes, and boils break out on their bodies. These plagues aren't random; they are targeted strikes against the false gods of Egypt, showing that the one true God holds power over creation itself. God isn't just freeing the Israelites. More than that, God is making a bold declaration to the entire world that there is no other God like him, and he stands on the side of God's people.

But even in the midst of these harsh judgments, there is mercy. God gives Pharaoh chance after chance to relent, to humble himself, and to release the Israelites. God's desire isn't just to destroy Egypt; it's to reveal his power so that all people might come to know him. God's justice is always wrapped in an invitation to repentance. In this season, when we are facing our own sinfulness and brokenness, this message becomes vital. This story forces us to confront a hard truth: God will fight for us, but he will also allow us to feel the consequences of our sinful and prideful decisions. Pharaoh's heart is hardened not only by God's actions but by his own refusal to surrender. How often do we find ourselves in the same place? How often does our pride keep us from bending the knee, from admitting that we need God?

We may not experience plagues like those in Egypt, but we know what it's like to feel the weight of our own stubbornness.

Broken relationships, missed opportunities, and spiritual dryness can all be the result of hearts unwilling to submit. God's discipline isn't meant to break us—it's meant to lead us back to God. The question is whether we will recognize God's mercy in the midst of everything else. The invitation of Lent is to surrender before the frogs arrive, before the water turns to blood. It's an invitation to humble ourselves daily, acknowledging that God is God and we are not. It's choosing to trust that even in the discomfort, God's power is always working for our good.

The good news is that God's desire isn't just to show God's power—it's to rescue an entire people. The same God who sends the plagues is the God who splits the sea, who leads his people to freedom, and who ultimately sends his Son to rescue us from the power of sin. Let that truth soften your heart today. God will fight for you, but God longs for you to come willingly into his arms.

- Where is pride quietly hardening your heart? Are there areas of your life where God is inviting you to surrender, but you've been holding on too tightly?
- Have you ever felt like God let you experience the consequences of your actions? What was that like? How did you react?

DAY 10

Exodus 10

Key Verses: 10:1-2

In our key verses for today, God reveals a deeper purpose behind the plagues. The immediate goal is clear: to force Pharaoh's hand and secure the release of the Hebrew slaves. But God's vision extends far beyond the present moment. The plagues are meant to leave a lasting impression, not just on Pharaoh and the Egyptians, but on the hearts of God's own people. God wants this story to be told and retold, passed down from generation to generation, as a powerful testimony to divine power and God's unwavering faithfulness.

This desire for the story to endure speaks to the very nature of God. God is not a distant deity, working in secret behind the scenes. God moves boldly and dynamically so that his people can see, remember, and proclaim his goodness. The liberation of the Israelites isn't just a one-time act of deliverance; it's the foundation of their entire identity as God's chosen people. Every miracle, every plague, every act of power is a signpost pointing to who God is and how deeply God loves his people.

But there's a heartbreaking pattern that plays out again and again in Scripture. As the years pass and generations shift, the stories begin to fade. When the Israelites forget what God has done, their hearts begin to wander. They seek meaning and security in other gods, falling into cycles of sin and disobedience. Each time, God must intervene, raising up judges, prophets, and kings to call the people back to faithfulness.

This pattern isn't unique to the Israelites. It's a human struggle that still plays out today. I have experienced this in myself and seen it with others. We experience some mountaintop moment, when God's goodness changes our lives, but as weeks and months pass, the feeling fades, and we slide back into old patterns. Where we once were quick to tell this story to friends and family, we allow this moment to fade back in our minds.

God's instructions to the Israelites are also relevant for us today. We are meant to be storytellers—people who bear witness to what God has done in our lives. Think about your own faith journey. When was the last time you shared with a young person about how God has moved in your life? How often do we talk about the ways God has answered prayers, provided in times of need, or carried us through difficult seasons? It's easy to lament the struggles of younger generations—their disconnection from the church, their shifting values, their search for identity in the wrong places. But before we point fingers, wc have to ask ourselves: Have we done our part? Have we been intentional about passing down the stories of God's goodness? Have we modeled a faith that is vibrant, honest, and alive?

Sharing our stories doesn't have to be complicated. It can be as simple as telling a child or grandchild about a time when God showed up in your life. It can be praying out loud with your family and letting them hear your gratitude and trust. It can be pointing out God's goodness in the small, everyday moments—the beauty of creation, the kindness of a stranger, the peace that comes in the chaos. Our stories have the power to shape the faith of those who come after us. When we testify to what God has done, we build a foundation of trust and hope for the next generation. We remind them that God is not just a figure from ancient history. Rather, God is alive and active, still working in the world and in our lives today. May we never stop telling the stories of what God has done, so that our children, grandchildren, and church family may know and believe that there is no one like the Lord our God.

- How can you tell the story of God's activity in your life to the children in your life?
- What story would you tell them? Think through it now so you can be ready to share when the opportunity arises.

DAY 11

Exodus 11

Key Verses: Exodus 11

It is time for the plagues to be over. God has displayed power far beyond Pharaoh's, proving again and again that no earthly ruler can rival the Almighty. The relentless back and forth between God and Pharaoh is coming to its final, devastating conclusion: the death of the firstborn sons of all Egypt. This final plague is difficult to read, harsh in its execution, and unsettling in its severity. It's natural to wrestle with such a brutal display of power and wonder why God would choose this path.

To understand this act, we have to look beyond the surface. The death of the firstborn is not just about punishment; it's about protection. Israel is God's firstborn. The people of Israel are God's hope for the future, the carriers of his covenant and the embodiment of his promises. Pharaoh, in his pride and cruelty, has threatened God's firstborn by enslaving them, brutalizing them, and attempting to snuff out their very existence. God's response is not one of detached wrath, but of fierce, protective love—the kind of love that will stop at nothing to rescue God's children.

When I think about this, it reminds me of a float trip I took with my parents on the Buffalo River. In the middle of the trip, we stumbled upon a black bear with two little cubs. Even though we were at a safe distance, the mother bear rose onto her hind legs and growled, making it clear that we were not to come any closer. Her strength and desire to protect were palpable, and even as a child, I understood the message: These cubs were precious, and she would not let anything happen to them. There is no reasoning with a mother bear when her young are in danger. She doesn't act out of malice but out of an instinctive, unwavering commitment to protect what is most precious to her. Her ferocity is not born from hatred, but from love.

God's actions in this story are rooted in that same protective passion. God is not acting out of a desire to destroy, but out of a holy determination to save his people. The full revelation of God's heart and desire to save comes through Jesus Christ, who shows us that God's ultimate weapon against evil is not death, but sacrificial love. While this story may challenge our understanding of God, it also invites us to see the unwavering commitment behind God's actions.

God stands between us and whatever threatens our well-being. The world is full of dangers, both seen and unseen, but we are never left to fend for ourselves. God stands guard over God's children with a love that is both tender and fierce. This image of God as our protector offers profound comfort. When life feels uncertain or when we face forces beyond our control, we can rest in the knowledge that we are not alone. God's protective love surrounds us, shielding us from harm and fighting battles we cannot see. That doesn't mean life will always be easy or that we'll be spared from every hardship, but it does mean that God's love is always at work, even in the midst of our struggles.

As we continue our Lenten journey, take a moment to reflect on the ways God has protected you. Can you remember a time when you felt God's presence standing between you and danger? Are there moments in your life when you only realized God's protection in hindsight? Let this story remind you that God's love is not passive or distant. It is active, present, and unyielding—like a mother bear watching over her cubs. May you find comfort in that truth today, knowing that the God who delivered Israel still watches over you with that same fierce and faithful love.

- Have you ever had reservations about God's treatment of the Egyptians? Do you think the Israelites might have? Does the image of God as a mother bear change how you think about God's actions?
- What other images or metaphors for God's protectiveness can you think of?

DAY 12

Exodus 12

Key Verses: 12:29-32

This passage from Exodus is one of the most challenging and sobering pieces of Scripture we encounter. It's not a lighthearted story; it's the culmination of a long struggle between God and Pharaoh, a battle that ends with the deaths of all the male firstborn of Egypt, including Pharaoh's own son. It's hard to process the sheer devastation of that night, what it must have felt like for the families who lost their loved ones and the heartbreak that filled Egypt. And yet, it is also one of the most important moments in the Bible, a turning point in God's plan.

The content of this passage is deeply unsettling, and I don't want to gloss over that. The cost of this deliverance is extreme. God's judgment falls on Egypt in a powerful, painful way. The death of the firstborn is a striking reminder of not only the high price of freedom but also the gravity of sin and rebellion. For Pharaoh, it was the result of a final act of defiance against God's will; for Israel, it was the sign of a decisive, redemptive act. There's no way to sugarcoat the violence of this moment, but we can trust in God's righteousness and justice. God is not unjust, even when the judgment is severe. God was working to overcome evil, to break the grip of slavery, and to secure freedom for the Israelites.

The Passover itself is a ritual of remembrance, a way for the Israelites to celebrate what God did for them and to mark a new beginning in their history. God instructs the Israelites to remember this night every year with the celebration of the Passover. Through eating and drinking in a certain way at an established time, a ritual is created— a ritual that tells the story of God's protection, salvation, and love. The meal becomes the vessel in which the truth of God's character is revealed and passed down from generation to generation. It's a beautiful image of God's mercy, protection, and provision in the midst of judgment.

And yet, as powerful as that moment was, it also points us toward something even greater, something that would unfold thousands of years later. When Jesus sat down with his disciples to celebrate the Passover, he took the bread and the wine and redefined them. No longer was the lamb's blood the focus; it was now his own blood, poured out for the forgiveness of sins. Jesus was fulfilling the ultimate sacrifice, offering himself as the Lamb of God who takes away the sin of the world.

This new covenant that Christ established is not one that requires the lives of our enemies. Instead, it's marked by the incredible grace of God, who didn't demand the death of anyone else but gave up his own Son for us. The price of freedom for us came at a tremendous cost, God himself paying the ultimate price so that we could be saved. In return, God asks for our repentant faithfulness, turning from our past sinfulness and recommitting ourselves to a mature and obedient life of faith. It's hard to imagine a starker contrast. The first Passover was a time of judgment and death, but in Christ, we find salvation and life. In him, God acted decisively to save his people not through judgment on others but through the willing sacrifice. The message of Passover, of God's deliverance, resonates throughout Scripture, culminating in the cross of Christ. We are reminded again and again that God's salvation comes at a high cost but also that God is always willing to pay it.

As we reflect on the Passover, let us remember both the severity of God's judgment and the depth of God's love. We celebrate God's victory over sin and death, but we also recognize the great cost of our redemption: God's victory over evil came through the greatest sacrifice of all. God saves. God has always saved and will always save.

- How do you understand God's action against Egypt's firstborn sons?
- Where do you need God to save you today? From what trial or temptation?

DAY 13

Exodus 13

Key Verses: 13:11-22

In today's passage from Exodus, two significant themes stand out, both of which lay the foundation for the greater story of redemption that unfolds throughout Scripture. The first is centered on the Hebrew word *pada*, which means "redeem." God commands that all firstborn males be consecrated to him, which many understand as requiring that they be given completely to God in some form of ritual sacrifice. But God allows for a substitution, offering families the option to give a lesser sacrifice in place of their firstborn.

This idea of substitution is a powerful one. It sets up a pattern that ultimately finds its fulfillment in Jesus. The sacrificial system was always meant to point to something greater—the sacrifice of Jesus, the Lamb of God, who would be offered in our place. He takes our place on the cross, paying the debt we could never repay. Just like those who offered sacrifices in Exodus 13, we, too, benefit from a substitutionary act of grace. God offers to pay our debt, a debt we could never hope to pay ourselves.

I'm sure you can think of moments in your life when someone showed incredible generosity, maybe a parent helping you out financially when you were in a bind or a friend covering for you in a tight spot. When my now wife, Mary, and I had just moved to Dallas for my seminary education, I got our first apartment. We were engaged and living separately, and I had spent every dime I had on dishes, bedding, and furniture. I had a job lined up, but I was weeks away from a paycheck. The pantry was as empty as my bank account, and I was unsure how I was going to get by.

The next day, Mary's dad came to visit, and Mary had secretly told him about my position. When he arrived, he greeted me with a handshake that contained six fresh $100 bills. I was saved by this act of extravagant generosity. Years later, Mary's father died, and the following Christmas, her mom gave us our last Christmas gift from their father. It was six $100 bills. This time, my situation was far different, but I took the money and created investment funds for each of our three kids—funds that one day can be their grandfather's way of saving them if they ever get in a tight spot. Such acts of kindness and moments of redemption point us to the ultimate act of redemption found in Christ. Just as God made a way for his people in Exodus to keep what they valued while still honoring God, so Christ offers himself in our place, paying the price that frees us.

The second major theme of this passage is God's constant and faithful leadership. God is not just the one who redeems his people; God is also the one who leads them. In this chapter, we see God going before the Israelites in a pillar of cloud by day and a pillar of fire by night, guiding them every step of the way toward the Promised Land. This is no ordinary leadership. God is present, visible, and active, leading his people with purpose and care. Even when he directs them away from potential conflict with the Philistines, he does so to protect them, not just physically but spiritually as well.

By avoiding the conflict, God keeps his people from turning back to Egypt, from longing for the security of their former enslavement. God's leadership in this moment is so profound. It's not just about guiding his people through the wilderness; it's about teaching them to trust in God, to follow God's lead, and to understand that God is enough to sustain them. God knows what they need and where they need to go, and he is actively involved in guiding them. God doesn't just deliver them from Egypt, but rather leads them toward something better.

While we may not see a physical pillar of cloud or fire today, God's leadership remains just as real. God still leads us day by day, guiding us through the challenges of life, providing for us, and reminding us that he is with us. We may not always see the way forward clearly, but God's presence is with us, just as it was with the Israelites.

God is still in front of us, leading us toward the promises he has for us. And God is also behind us, protecting us and making sure we don't turn back to the security of our old ways, our former slavery to sin. We are reminded in this passage that God is both our redeemer and our leader. God's redemption comes at a cost, but it is a cost God is willing to pay. God's leadership is steady, unwavering, and loving. Just as God led the Israelites into the Promised Land, God continues to lead us toward the fullness of his promises in Christ. And along the way, God offers us guidance, protection, and faithfulness, reminding us that we don't have to walk this journey alone.

- How have you experienced God's redeeming work in your life, paying a debt you could not afford to pay?
- How can you pay better attention to the leadership of God in your life? Name two practices you could use each day to help you better see and hear God's guidance.

DAY 14

Exodus 14

Key Verses: 14:10-14

The parting of the Red Sea is undoubtedly one of the most famous and awe-inspiring stories in the Book of Exodus. It's a moment that captures our imagination as God makes a way through the waters for his people. But as incredible as that moment is, I believe the events leading up to the parting of the Red Sea are just as remarkable. In fact, it's what happens before the waters are parted that reveals the depth of God's faithfulness and the profound transformation that still needs to take place in the hearts of the Israelites.

As the Israelites flee Egypt, they come to the edge of the Red Sea, only to see the Egyptian army closing in behind them. The approaching army is a terrifying, seemingly inescapable threat. To the Israelites, it looks like certain death. They are cornered, completely vulnerable, and they believe they have no way out. Their immediate response is to cry out to God—a reaction that, in many ways, has become typical for them. But if we listen closely, we'll hear something different in their cry. It's not just a plea for deliverance; it's an accusation. They begin to ask Moses three pointed questions, and each question references Egypt. In fact, they mention Egypt five times in their accusations. Egypt is the only place they truly know. Egypt has shaped their identity, and in this moment, they are still defined by their past captivity.

The people's words reveal the struggle they are facing. They would rather return to the security of slavery in Egypt than risk their lives attempting to embrace the freedom God has promised them. The bitterness of their past is still more familiar to them than the faithfulness of God. They are not yet fully trusting in Yahweh. Their hearts are still bound by the chains of Egypt, and they can't yet comprehend the greatness of the God who has brought them this far.

Moses, however, responds with the good news. He doesn't get caught up in their accusations or their fear. Instead, he offers them a reassuring imperative: "Do not be afraid, stand firm, and see the deliverance that the Lord will accomplish for you today" (v. 13). Moses refuses to view the situation as a conflict between Israel and Egypt alone. To him, it's not about Israel versus Egypt—it's about Israel and God versus Egypt. God is at the center of this story, not the Israelites' complaints or fear.

Moses reminds the people of God's faithfulness. He points them back to the plagues that led them out of Egypt, the signs and wonders that demonstrated God's power and commitment to their freedom. But most importantly, Moses delivers a statement that echoes through the ages: "The Lord will fight for you, and you have only to keep still" (verse 14). In other words, Moses says, "Sit back, stop complaining, and remember the power of the God you serve." The battle is not theirs to fight. The deliverance is not something they can accomplish by their own strength or effort. All they need to do is trust in the one who has already proven his faithfulness time and time again. In a world and a culture that values movement of any kind over stillness, this message rings loudly. When I think that I need to act or do to solve some problem or fix some issue, I am reminded that there are moments when God needs me to be still instead.

I'm also particularly moved by this moment because, at this point, the waters haven't even parted. The Israelites are still standing on the edge of the sea with the Egyptian army approaching, and yet Moses speaks with confidence and authority. He doesn't just tell them to stop complaining; he tells them to trust, to trust in the one who has brought them this far and will not abandon them now. The situation may look bleak, but God is still in control. The Israelites are about to see something that will forever change their perspective on God's power and faithfulness. But even before the waters part, Moses calls them to remember and rest in the truth of God's presence with them.

It's easy to get caught up in our own fears and worries, especially when we're faced with seemingly insurmountable obstacles. Like the Israelites, we often look back at what is familiar—what feels secure—even if it's not what God has promised for us. But Moses's words ring out to us today: "Do not be afraid, stand firm, and see the deliverance." Trust in the God who fights for us, who has already won the victory on our behalf. We are called not to fight on our own, but to rest in God's faithfulness, knowing that God will make a way where there seems to be no way.

- Why do you think it is hard for us to sit still and let the Lord fight for us? Why is it hard for you specifically?
- God's ultimate victory over the armies of Egypt were a signal to the world of God's might. Where do you see the signs of God's power in your life?

DAY 15

Exodus 15

Key Verses: 15:13-21

Today, we transition from the action-packed narrative of the Exodus to a moment of celebration—two beautiful songs of worship and praise that flow out of the people's experience of deliverance. Moses and all of Israel sing the first song, and Miriam, Moses's sister, sings the second, accompanied by all the other women dancing in celebration. These songs are more than just expressions of joy; they reveal something about the nature of God and our response to God's greatness.

As we look closely at verses 13-17, it's important to keep in mind the context that precedes them. The Israelites have just crossed through the Red Sea, narrowly escaping the pursuing Egyptian army. Before they even reach safety, they begin to sing. The opening of the song is focused on praising God's strength and power—attributes that are worthy of worship. But then the song shifts. It's no longer just about God's strength in battle; it also celebrates God's steadfast love, God's faithfulness as a guide and protector. The people of Israel, freshly delivered, recognize that it is not just God's might that has saved them, but God's love.

So often, we tend to view God in one of two extremes. We may focus on God as judge, creator, or warrior—powerful and mighty, which are certainly aspects of who God is. But what happens when we need comfort? Or encouragement? Or teaching? If we only understand God in one dimension, it becomes difficult to see God as the gentle shepherd or the loving Father when we need that tenderness. The song of Moses and Israel helps us see the multifaceted nature of God—strength and might, yes, but also love and care. God is not one-dimensional. God is the creator and the comforter, the judge and the savior. This song invites us to connect with every part of who God is, recognizing that God is always with us, whether in times of triumph or in moments when we need guidance.

The second important lesson here is the role of worship in responding to God's goodness. The Israelites' first action after crossing the Red Sea and experiencing God's deliverance is to worship. They don't rush off to rest or celebrate in any other way—they immediately begin to praise God. This moment of real safety, after the fear and uncertainty they've just lived through, calls for worship. It's a powerful reminder to us of how worship should flow naturally from our own experiences of God's goodness. We, too, should respond to God's faithfulness with hearts full of praise and gratitude.

I can't help but imagine what this moment must have looked like: six hundred thousand men and women (12:37), singing and dancing together in exuberant worship. Can you picture it? What a sight it must have been to see the entire community united in worship after such a dramatic deliverance. This is a moment of pure joy, and it's a reminder to us that worship is not just a quiet, solemn experience. It is also loud, joyful, and celebratory. Worship is a response to God's action in our lives, and it calls for everything we've got—our voices, our bodies, and our hearts.

Let's capture some of that enthusiasm the next time we gather to worship together. Whether it's in a corporate setting or a personal moment of reflection, may we remember that our worship is a natural response to the goodness of God. When we take time to reflect on God's deliverance, love, and faithfulness, the only proper response is worship. And it should be filled with joy, energy, and praise!

- What facet of God's persona do you typically see? Which is a struggle for you to connect with? Why?
- What would worship look like for you if you brought the same energy as these newly freed slaves? How would it change your experience and the church in general?

DAY 16

Exodus 16

Key Verses: 16:4-15

Before we dive into today's reading, I feel as though we need to clarify something. Over the next ten days or so, the Israelites are going to sound like whiny toddlers in need of a nap, constantly complaining about their lot in life and blaming Moses and God for it. It can be easy for us, those who aren't in their shoes, to wonder how they could possibly have so little trust in God to lead them after all they had seen. But the truth is the trauma they experienced in slavery powerfully impacted their hearts and minds, and the slightest threat sends them into panic mode. Additionally, how often have you and I failed to trust God's providence in our lives or failed to be obedient? Understanding this will help us get less frustrated with them when they complain again and again.

That being said, they complain this time about a lack of food. In Egypt, they had a secure, if meager, source of food. But now, in the wilderness, they are unsure how they will survive. God does not meet their anxiety with punishment for their lack of faith; instead, God responds with provision. God takes over the complaint hurled at Moses and offers a solution. He will provide them with manna (a sort of bread) and quail from heaven, just enough for each day. On the sixth day, they receive enough to cover the seventh, showing them how to trust God for their daily needs.

But here's the catch: There will be a test. Can the Israelites reorder their understanding of who is truly sovereign? Food, in Egypt, had to be hoarded. It was scarce, and the people lived in constant fear of running out. But God wants to transform their perspective. This food comes from God's storehouses, not from Pharaoh's. God wants them to shed the fear that drives that hoarding mentality. God wants them to trust that there will always be enough, that God's provision is consistent and sufficient.

What if we were forced to live off manna for the next forty years, relying each day upon God to feed and nourish us? Wouldn't we become more trusting, more reliant, and more faithful? I think we would. But isn't that what we do already? Everything we have comes from God, but because it's so consistent, so regular, we sometimes fail to see the miraculous nature of our daily bread. Augustine, reflecting on Jesus's miracle of turning water into wine at the wedding in Cana, offers a profound insight:

> The miracle indeed of our Lord Jesus Christ, whereby He made the water into wine, is not marvelous to those who know that it was God's doing. For He who made wine on

> that day at the marriage feast, in those six water-pots, which He commanded to be filled with water, the self-same does this every year in vines. For even as that which the servants put into the water-pots was turned into wine by the doing of the Lord, so in like manner also is what the clouds pour forth changed into wine by the doing of the same Lord. But we do not wonder at the latter, because it happens every year: it has lost its marvelousness by its constant recurrence.[1]

In other words, everything we eat comes from God, but because it doesn't feel miraculous every time we eat, we fail to recognize the miracle of God's provision. The sun rises every day. Rain falls every year. Bread is on our table every morning. Yet in these regular gifts, God is still working wonders, providing for us day by day. We often forget to marvel at God's goodness simply because it's so constant. I believe the key to deepening our trust in God is a simple attitude shift paired with heightened intentionality. If we begin to see our daily bread not just as sustenance but as a miracle, we will grow more reliant, more trusting, and more faithful. Just as the Israelites had to learn to trust that God would provide for their needs, we, too, are invited to trust in God's daily provision for us. It may not always feel like a dramatic miracle, but it is a miracle all the same.

- How often do you think about where your food actually comes from? Try really thinking about all the processes and people involved in getting food to your kitchen and give thanks to God for each of them.

- Reread the quote from St. Augustine. How do his words stir you? What things that God provides do you take for granted?

1 St. Augustine, *Homilies on the Gospel of John* in vol. 7 of *Nicene and Post-Nicene Fathers of the Christian Church*, ed. Philip Schaff, trans. John Gibb and James Innes (New York: The Christian Literature Company, 1888), 57.

DAY 17

Exodus 17

Key Verses: 17:8-13

I warned you about the complaining Israelites, did I not? And if you recall from yesterday, we spoke about understanding their frustration and struggles as they journeyed through the wilderness. Today, we're diving into two stories that show God's faithful protection and his very real presence with his people. While the Israelites' complaints are still very much ongoing, the focus here shifts to how God moves in miraculous ways to provide for and protect them, even when their faith wavers.

First, let's look at the dramatic scene in which Moses strikes the rock with his staff and water begins to gush out in the middle of the desert. This is one of those images that sticks with you: Moses, in the dry, barren wilderness, doing something that doesn't make sense, and yet, through his obedience, God provides for the people. The water that flows from that rock is life-giving.

For us, it's hard to grasp the intensity of that moment unless you've truly experienced dehydration or a lack of clean water. I've spent my share of long days working hard under the Arkansas summer sun, and I can tell you there's nothing more refreshing than a drink of ice-cold water from a five-gallon bucket. Imagine the Israelites, all of them parched and tired, desperate for water, and in that moment, God answers. I'm sure the relief was immense. It's a simple but profound miracle: God provides for his people in their time of need, in a way that they could not have been predicted or anticipated.

As the Israelites drink, we also meet Joshua, though this time, his military skill is not the focus. Instead, we see his faith and his dependence on God as a leader. He's tasked with leading Israel's army against the Amalekites, and as the battle unfolds, something crucial is revealed: The victory is directly tied to God's presence. Moses stands on a hill overlooking the battlefield, and as long as he keeps his hands raised, the Israelites prevail. But as Moses grows tired, his hands fall, and the Amalekites begin to have the advantage. It's in this moment of weakness that Aaron and Hur step in, holding Moses's hands up until the battle is won.

This powerful image is a reminder that the success of God's people doesn't come from their own strength or strategies, but from the presence of God among them. It's so tangible—when Moses's hands are raised, Israel triumphs. This story is a clear illustration that it's not human effort that brings victory, but God's power. The Israelites may have been able to fight a physical battle, but it was only God's presence and intervention that gave them the strength to win. They didn't earn that victory—they received it as a gift from a faithful and present God.

Now, I have to admit, I can't help but feel frustrated by the Israelites at times. How could they be so quick to forget all that God had done for them, especially when God's presence was so obviously in front of them? How could they question God's ability to provide after all the miraculous ways God had already shown up for them?

But when I look at my own life, I realize that I, too, often fail to recognize the ways God is actively working, even when it's happening right in front of me. God's work in our lives today might not look as dramatic as parting the Red Sea or bringing water from a rock, but God is just as faithful and just as present. In my own lifetime, God's activity has often been behind the scenes, working through people and circumstances in ways that don't always feel miraculous. Sometimes, I long for those visible, obvious signs of God's presence—a pillar of fire or a cloud leading me through the day—but the reality is that God is present in the quiet moments, in the stillness, and through the Holy Spirit, guiding us in unseen ways. It's easy to wish for something more tangible, but what we need to do is open our eyes to see Jesus in the here and now. He is with us, even when we don't feel his presence in the dramatic, visible ways we might expect.

The key takeaway from these stories is that God's presence is the ultimate source of strength and provision for his people.

The Israelites could do nothing without God's intervention, and neither can we. In times of difficulty, when life feels like a battle or when we're thirsty in the wilderness, we can trust that God will provide for us, just as God provided for the Israelites. God's faithfulness and presence never waver. While we may not have the same visible signs, we can still rely on the truth that God is here, with us, leading and providing in ways we might not always see but can always trust. When we grow tired, when our hands drop in exhaustion, God is the one holding us up.

- Have you ever felt frustration at the Israelites in this story or at people in your own life who don't seem able to see what God is doing for them? What is the best response to witnessing this kind of reaction?
- How can you open your heart to see God more clearly today?

DAY 18

Exodus 18

Key Verses: 18:21-22

There's something unique about a father-in-law who's been around the block a few times and knows a thing or two about the challenges life can bring. Even more unique is one who is willing to step in and offer assistance to a son-in-law in need. Jethro, Moses's father-in-law, sees the stress and burden that Moses is carrying as he tries to lead the Israelites through the wilderness. In a moment of wisdom, Jethro offers a piece of advice that not only relieves Moses but shapes the leadership structure for the people of Israel for generations to come. It's a perfect example of someone stepping in with clarity and counsel, recognizing a problem, and offering a solution.

Jethro's advice to Moses is simple yet profound: You cannot do it all alone. Moses needs to delegate responsibilities to others who can help carry the load. The focus of this story isn't about the details of this new political structure, but rather on who would fill these roles. These leaders weren't to be picked based on their wealth, tribal status, or social standing. Instead, Jethro focuses on character. His recommendation is clear: Choose capable, godly leaders who will uphold the values of integrity, fairness, and justice.

In verses 21-22, we see the specific qualities Jethro looks for in these leaders. The first is practical competency. In verse 21, the call to find "able" men is a translation of the Hebrew word *hayil*, which means individuals who are resourceful, skilled, and capable of managing responsibilities. These leaders need to be able to handle the weight of the task and make wise decisions for the people. It is clear that God doesn't care about titles or positions of power; rather, God wants those who possess the heart and mind to lead well.

Next, Jethro insists that these leaders must "fear God. " Moses needs leaders who share a healthy respect and reverence for God. It was impossible for the Hebrews to deny God's power and might, and these new leaders must continue to instill that truth in the people. Keeping this truth fresh in the hearts and minds of Israel would build their trust in God and God's continued activity in their lives.

The third characteristic is trustworthiness. Jethro emphasizes that these leaders must be reliable and have a public track record that reflects honesty and character. Trust is the cornerstone of any leadership role. People need to know that the leaders they follow can be counted on to tell the truth, to act with integrity, and to lead with justice. This speaks to the kind of consistency and character that must be proven over time, not just in moments of convenience but especially in times of difficulty.

Finally, Jethro says that these leaders must "hate dishonest gain." They must actively despise corruption, bribery, and any form of deceitfulness that undermines justice. These leaders must stand firm against the temptation to compromise their values, and they must actively protect the integrity of the judicial process. In a world where power and influence can so easily be corrupted, Jethro's instructions are a call to uphold righteousness, no matter the cost.

Have you ever experienced leadership like Jethro calls for? How did it make you feel to follow someone who you could trust, who you knew was leading with integrity and faithfulness? How would you feel if someone you respected described you in this way? Capable, godly, trustworthy, and just—aren't these qualities we should all strive for?

It's easy to get caught up in the busyness of life and overlook the importance of integrity, but at the heart of good leadership is character. It's not just about being able to get things done; it's about doing things the right way. We may not be in charge of a nation like Moses, but we all have areas where we can embody these qualities. Let's seek to live in the footsteps of these early leaders of Israel and ask God to refine our character to reflect God's values in all we do.

- Have you had leaders who embody the qualities Jethro calls for? What was that experience like?
- In what areas of your life can you seek to embody these characteristics?
- Which of these characteristics do you think comes most naturally to you? Which one do you need to work on the most to develop?

DAY 19

Exodus 19

Key Verses: 19:4-9

Covenant. It is one of the most important themes running throughout the Book of Exodus and indeed throughout the whole of God's relationship with humanity. A covenant is more than a contract; it is a sacred agreement between two parties in which each side makes a promise to do certain things and behave in certain ways. Unlike a human contract, which is based on equal give-and-take, a covenant with God is wholly unique because one of the parties is the Lord of all creation. God, with infinite grace, always gives far more than he asks in return. This is God's chosen way of being in relationship with us, promising to be a constant source of life, strength, and salvation while asking us to be faithful and obedient in return.

Here in Exodus 19, we witness a profound moment of covenant-making between God and the freed Israelites. God reminds them of what he has already done—how he carried them "on eagles' wings" out of Egypt and brought them to himself. The imagery here is of protection, care, and divine deliverance. Now,

God sets before them a future full of promise. The Israelites will be his special people, blessed to be a blessing. The people, moved by the grandeur of God's presence and the weight of God's words, respond with a unanimous agreement: "Everything the Lord has spoken, we will do." The covenant is then ratified through consecration, and God prepares to reveal himself in fullness and might upon Mount Sinai.

This moment in Israel's history holds echoes for us today. We, too, are in a covenant relationship with God. Through Christ, we are invited into the new covenant, one in which our part is clear: to believe in Jesus; to love the Lord our God with all our heart, soul, mind, and strength; and to love our neighbors as ourselves. But how often do we truly think about our faith as a covenant? How often do we approach our relationship with God with the same weight of commitment that Israel was called to have at Sinai?

I think we struggle to really grasp the idea of covenant because so many of our relationships feel more like contracts than faithful covenants. We agree to love and value our friends as long as they are nice to us, invite us along to things, and help us when we need it. But if they were to become too busy for us or were less interesting or fun, we might be quick to void the contract and end the relationship. Unfortunately, we have the ability to allow our hearts to treat our spouses, parents, children, and friends like service providers rather than beloved children of God who we have the chance to deeply love and serve. God is calling us into covenant and to use this relationship as a model for how we are to be in relationship with others.

God has already upheld his end of the covenant: He has redeemed us, provided for us, and invited us into a relationship. Now, it is up to us to remain faithful, to listen to the voice of the Holy Spirit, and to walk daily in obedience. May we, like the Israelites, respond with commitment: "Everything the Lord has spoken, we will do." And may we follow through, not just in word but in action, living each day as people of the covenant.

- Thinking deeply about this idea of a covenant relationship with God, what areas of your life might need work or renewal?
- How can you strengthen your covenant relationship today? How can you be more obedient to God's guidance?

DAY 20

Exodus 20

Key Verses: 20:1-17

The Ten Commandments. Its words are foundational, the very core of what it means to live as God's people. For thousands of years, they have stood as a guide for moral living, shaping societies and influencing countless laws and ethical systems. Even those who do not claim the Christian faith often recognize their importance. But for us as believers, they are more than just rules; they are the heartbeat of a covenant relationship between God and God's people.

I will admit that much of my ministry has centered on preaching the radical grace of God—the beautiful, unshakable truth that God loves us always, no matter what. I stand by this core tenet of our faith. However, as I reflect more on these commandments, I recognize that I do not give enough thought to the danger of sin. We are quick to talk about grace, and rightly so, but sometimes slow to acknowledge that sin has real and devastating consequences. God's grace is not a free pass to live however we choose. The Ten Commandments exist not as arbitrary rules designed to restrict us but as divine guidelines meant to protect us from the destructive power of sin.

Each commandment is rooted in love, the love for God and love for one another. The first four focus on our relationship with God: placing God above all else, rejecting idolatry, honoring God's name, and keeping the Sabbath as a holy day of rest and worship. These commandments set the foundation for the rest, because when we align our hearts with God's will, it naturally flows into how we treat others. The final six commandments govern our relationships with people: honoring parents, refraining from murder, adultery, theft, false witness, and covetousness. They remind us that our faith is not just about personal piety, but about how we live in community. What appears to be on the surface a series of disconnected rules becomes a gorgeously woven tapestry of a life faithfully lived.

When I learned the Ten Commandments as a child, I thought that following them would be easy. I wasn't killing anyone or coveting anyone else's wife. But as I grew in faith I learned that Jesus challenges us in the Sermon on the Mount by expanding these laws beyond mere outward actions to the condition of our hearts. He teaches that anger toward another person can be just as harmful as murder, that lustful thoughts are as destructive as adultery, and that honesty must go beyond not lying—it must be a way of life.

This is where the rubber of the Ten Commandments meets the road of righteous living. We must not just avoid sin but actively seek to live as faithfully as possible. When we choose faithfulness over idolatry, contentment over covetousness, truth over deception, and love over selfishness, we reflect the character of God.

I am particularly struck by how countercultural these commandments are in today's world. We live in a society that often celebrates self-interest, materialism, and moral ambiguity. The world tells us that success is found in wealth, power, and personal gratification. But the Ten Commandments call us to a different way of living—a way marked by reverence for God, respect for others, and integrity in all things.

As we seek to live out the Ten Commandments today, we remember that Jesus summed up the entire law with two commands: Love the Lord your God with all your heart, soul, mind, and strength, and love your neighbor as yourself. To live this way, we must also be intentional about examining our hearts. Are there areas where we have allowed compromise? Do we place our career, money, or relationships above God? Do we justify small lies or harbor resentment toward others? The commandments are not outdated relics; they are living truths that still hold us accountable today.

Finally, we need to remember that while the law reveals sin, grace empowers us to live righteously. We will fall short—we all do. But through Jesus Christ, we have the gift of forgiveness and the power of the Holy Spirit to transform our lives. The commandments remind us of our need for a Savior, and Jesus fulfills that need completely.

- Do you feel like you focus more on gratefulness for God's grace or a need of forgiveness for your sinfulness? Why do you think that is?
- How can you balance an appreciation for redemption with striving to stay away from sinful behavior?

DAY 21

Exodus 21

Key Verses: 21:2, 12-19

I think one of the things that I am most uncomfortable with is chaos. When things are seemingly beyond my control, when there is no discernible plan in sight, and when no one seems to be calling the shots, I find myself feeling anxious and unsettled. I don't like these situations, and I bet you are the same way. We long for order, for structure, for a sense of direction. This isn't just a personality trait that some of us possess; it's part of how we are created. God desires order, and as we are made in God's image, so do we.

That is why, before the Israelites even get settled in the Promised Land, God is already outlining for them the rules and principles that will shape them into a just and functioning society. The laws given in Exodus 21 and after may seem foreign to us today, sometimes even harsh. They may strike us as outdated, raising questions about their relevance in our modern world. But if we look closely, we begin to see something deeper at play: These laws reveal something essential about God's heart and character.

Take, for example, the laws about slavery. At first glance, it may be jarring to read about regulations on this rather than outright condemnation of the practice. But we must remember that the context of the ancient world was vastly different from our own. For what it's worth, the kind of slavery Exodus speaks about is not the race-based chattel slavery we are most familiar with from the history of the Americas. Rather, it was more akin to indentured servitude. And these laws place limits on that servitude, ensuring that it is not a permanent state but one with defined terms and rights. This demonstrates God's refusal to allow his people to be enslaved in the way they were in Egypt. He calls them to be different, to create a society where people are treated with dignity and fairness.

Then there are the laws regarding violence. The penalties may seem severe—death for striking or cursing a parent, for example—but these laws underscore the immense value that God places on human life. Life is sacred. It is not to be threatened or taken lightly. The laws in this chapter establish a society where people are held accountable for their actions, where life and justice matter, and where order is upheld so that the weak are not trampled by the strong. These laws reflect the character of God by outlining the kind of community that God desires.

So how should we engage with these laws today? First, we recognize that the heart of the law remains unchanged: God desires justice, mercy, and respect for human dignity. Jesus affirms this when he summarizes the law by telling us to "love your neighbor as yourself" (Mark 12:31). These laws, even the ones that seem strange to us, serve as a framework for how to treat others with honor and respect.

As we read them today, we can reflect on how these laws would influence the way that we treat others. I admit that some of them, including some of what we will read in the coming days, seem to have little bearing on our lives. Indeed, the way our society functions has changed radically since the Exodus, but the heart of God has not; how God wants us to be in relationship with himself and others remains the same. My hope is that as we study these laws, we don't simply see them as relics of the past but as reflections of the heart of a God who calls us to love, respect, and uphold the dignity of every person. May we strive to live in that love today and always.

- What value do you see in the Israelites' law beyond the Ten Commandments? What is its relevance for you today?
- How can you love someone else better today than you have in the past? What changes can you make in your behavior?
- How can you be more willing to submit to God's wisdom, even when it challenges your own understanding?

DAY 22

EXODUS 22

Key Verses: 22:21-24

This chapter might seem like a patient look at the mundane matters of life—property disputes, social responsibilities, and ethical business practices. But it is precisely in these everyday details that the health and well-being of a community are gained or lost. No matter the depth of our faithfulness, we still spend most of our time at work, in meetings or with budgets; at home, cooking dinner or mowing the grass; or spending time with friends and family, enjoying their company and squabbling over whose football team is better. The way that we do these things as disciples matters greatly to God.

What strikes me the most as I read through this chapter is that the God of all creation, the same God who parted the Red Sea, defeated Pharaoh, and led his people through the wilderness, cares about the ordinary aspects of human life. God isn't just concerned with the big picture; God is also deeply invested in how the people interact with one another in the day-to-day. That means God cares about the little moments in your life too. The next time you pour a cup of coffee, run a load of dishes, or help a neighbor, know that God sees you in those moments. I have often felt God in the most difficult and joyous moments but at the same time fail to recognize God when the alarm clock goes off or when I am tying my shoes. Yet God is with us in the routine, the ordinary, and the overlooked.

One of the most powerful themes in this chapter is God's unwavering concern for justice and deep compassion for the vulnerable. Over and over in Scripture, we see that God stands on the side of the poor, the marginalized, and the oppressed. Here, the laws specifically protect resident aliens, widows, and orphans. These people were, and often still are, at the highest risk of being taken advantage of. Widows and orphans had lost their male advocate, which left them particularly vulnerable, and God makes it clear that their mistreatment will not be tolerated. The message cannot be missed: God hears the cries of the oppressed and will act in their defense.

This should serve as a strong reminder to us today. If we claim to be followers of Christ, then our lives should reflect the same heart for justice that God demonstrates in Exodus 22. That means we must be mindful of how our actions—both intentional and unintentional—impact those around us. Are we speaking in ways that build others up or tear them down? Are we using our influence to help those in need or are we ignoring them? Are we ensuring that our communities reflect the kind of justice and mercy that God desires?

This passage reminds us that obedience to God is not just about avoiding sin; it is about actively working for good. It is about being people of justice, compassion, and generosity. The same God who cared about these details for Israel cares about them for us today. May we be people who take this to heart, living out God's love in the ordinary moments and standing up for those in need whenever we have the chance.

- If God cares about the mundane goings on in your life, how can you use those moments to get closer to God?
- How can you do a better job of standing on the side of the poor and oppressed where you live?

DAY 23

Exodus 23

Key Verses: 23:12-13

I am pretty sure we could spend three or four days in this chapter. There is so much for us to glean about the heart of God, from the lessons on upholding justice at all costs to the outlining of annual festivals and opportunities to celebrate and worship God. That doesn't even touch on the way that God shares with the people how they will enter into the Promised Land and the way God will continue to fight for them as they step into that land. I would strongly encourage you to read this whole chapter, and not just the key verses, because every section is packed with wisdom that is just as relevant for us today as it was for the Israelites then.

But those key verses are astounding in the way they highlight the importance of a day of rest. The sabbath day is not just a good idea or a helpful practice—it is a divine gift, a commandment from God directly. Let us compare this gift of God to the Hebrew's lives under Pharaoh's oppressive rule, where the people were worked to exhaustion without relief. But here, in the wilderness, God gives the opportunity to rest, to be refreshed, to remember they are more than the work they do.

For us, sabbath is more than just a day off. It is a test of loyalty. We are not forced to work by some tyrannical dictator, but we do find ourselves in a system where our value and meaning are often tied to career and earning potential. A faithful question then arises: Can we set aside our need to be productive for just one day and simply delight in the Lord? Can we stop long enough to remember that our value is not tied to what we earn, what we produce, or how much money we have? The world tells us that our identity is built on our achievements, but sabbath calls us to a different reality, one in which our worth is found solely in God.

This is why we need to take sabbath seriously. It is not just about recharging our batteries or getting a break from our busy schedules. It is about realigning our priorities, reminding ourselves that we belong to God, and trusting that God will provide for us even when we step away from our work. In observing sabbath, we declare our dependence on God rather than on our own ability to control our lives.

So, find your time to rest this week, my friends. Whether it be on Sunday or any other day, set aside intentional time to be still before God. Use it not just to relax but to worship, to reflect, and to remember your worth in God's loving gaze. Let sabbath be a sacred time in your week when you let go of the demands of the world and embrace the peace that only God can give.

- How can you be better at taking your sabbath time seriously?
- If Sunday doesn't work for you, what other time could you set aside for God?

DAY 24

Exodus 24

Key Verses: 24:3-8

The covenant between God and Israel is officially ratified in this passage. What began in Exodus 19, now finds its confirmation as the people commit themselves to God in a profound and solemn way. Up to this point, the Israelites have largely been passive participants in the story—recipients of God's deliverance, provision, and instruction. But here, something shifts. This is their first true sign of agency—a collective decision to bind themselves to God, to acknowledge their role in this divine relationship. This marks them as a people set apart, formed by the power and for the pleasure of the Holy One. Their belonging and cohesion are not dictated by human constructs but by a divine calling.

This idea of a covenant people extends beyond the pages of Exodus and speaks to our lives today. In a world that often feels disconnected, isolated, and transient, we are called to community, to belong to one another and to God.

Loneliness is an epidemic in modern society. Research shows that those who experience chronic loneliness are at a significantly higher risk of health problems, both mental and physical. In fact, in 2023, the US surgeon general released a report titled Our Epidemic of Loneliness and Isolation that details the negative outcomes associated with declining rates of social connection in the United States. The report notes that social isolation is about as dangerous to human life as smoking fifteen cigarettes each day, to say nothing of the emotional toll it can take.[1] When people have no one to turn to, no one to listen, encourage, or support them, the stresses, strains, and uncertainties of life are magnified with devastating results.

Perhaps one of the greatest lessons we can take from this passage is that true community is not just something we stumble upon; it is something we actively commit to. What if we saw our own church communities in this light? What if we broadened our definition of family to include those who walk this faith journey with us? What if our church members were not just people we see on Sunday mornings but true brothers and sisters, aunts and uncles, nieces and nephews in faith?

God's vision for community is one of deep connection and intentional commitment. It is not about mere social gatherings or surface-level friendships. It is about a shared covenant, a mutual decision to love, support, and walk with one another in faith. The Israelites understood that to follow God meant to walk together as a people, and the same is true for us today.

Take a moment to reflect on your own sense of community. Who are the people that make up your spiritual family? Are there individuals in your church or neighborhood who may be feeling isolated, longing for connection? Perhaps today is an opportunity to reach out—to extend an invitation, share a meal, or simply let others know they are not alone. In doing so, we live out the truth of God's covenant, not just as individuals but as a people bound together by God's love and faithfulness.

- Do you see people in your church as part of your family? What does being part of a church family mean to you and what can you do to bring people closer?
- What would change in your church if people were more connected? What would stay the same?

---

1 Office of the Surgeon General, *Our Epidemic of Loneliness and Isolation: The US Surgeon General's Advisory on the Healing Effects of Social Connection and Community*, (US Department of Health and Human Services, 2023), 25.

DAY 25

Exodus 25

Key Verses: 25:1-8

Shakan, the Hebrew word for "dwell," carries incredible meaning and significance here. On one hand, it signifies God's desire to be an abiding presence with the Israelites. God is at home in the midst of Israel. "Dwell" does not mean to sit permanently; rather, it suggests a presence that is active and intentional. God still has freedom and autonomy to be elsewhere, yet God chooses to be with the people. This moment is a profound turning point, as God establishes the pathway by which he can be with them in a unique and special way while also maintaining power as the creator and sustainer of all things.

This is an act of divine generosity. God, in all holiness and majesty, makes a way to be present among a people. This transition is striking when we reflect on the journey so far. We have seen God as the mighty deliverer, the warrior who overthrew the Egyptians, who parted the Red Sea, and who has created community through law giving. Now, the tone shifts. The same powerful God now speaks as a loving and nurturing presence, inviting Israel into a deeper relationship—one built not on fear, but on communion and trust.

The entire project of constructing a sacred place for God's presence begins with an offering from the people of Israel. This is a striking detail. God does not force them into building a dwelling place or simply provide them with one. Instead, God invites them to participate in the creation of a space worthy of God's presence. This means that establishing a place for God is human work, but it must be done with a spirit of generosity and willingness. Only those whose hearts are moved are called to give. This is not a tax or a demand but an opportunity, an invitation to those who desire true communion with God.

Their gift should be from the best they have, and as former slaves their best comes from the very materials they likely acquired from the Egyptians: gold, silver, bronze, fine linens, and precious stones. These spoils of God's conquering of the Egyptians are now repurposed for the glory of God. What was once a symbol of their past oppression and suffering is now transformed into an offering of devotion and gratitude.

In the same way, God longs to dwell with us today. But just as the Israelites had to prepare a place for him, we too must offer our best in order to make room for God in our lives. This is not about physical space but the space in our hearts, in our schedules, in our priorities. If we cling too tightly to the power, wealth, and distractions of this world, we leave little room for God to reign. Yet when we open our hands, when we give freely, when we offer up the best of ourselves—our time, our talents, our love—God comes and dwells with us in a way that transforms us completely.

I will never forget hearing from a busy mother who had exchanged her important career for raising her children and managing her household full time. She expressed that both roles kept her moving at a rapid pace, always feeling like there weren't enough hours in the day, whether she was in the boardroom or the playroom. Feeling exhausted physically and spiritually, she gave her heart over to God in desperation. God met her in her moment of weakness, and she gave what little she had left for God to use. After that moment, she began to see her daily tasks as gifts from God, opportunities to love her family and make a lasting impact in their lives. She recognized her value as a child of God and found energy and excitement in her work. This is what happens when we allow our hearts to dwell with God and God to dwell in us.

- In what ways can you offer your best to God and to make room for God to dwell with you?
- What parts of your life do you struggle to offer up to God? Money? Time? Energy? Why? How could God use those things for glory?

DAY 26

Exodus 26

Key Verses: 26:33-35

OK, friends, I'm just going to be up front with you. The next five days are probably not going to carry the same excitement as the first half of our Exodus journey. We've moved past the dramatic moments of deliverance from Egypt, the parting of the Red Sea, and the powerful moments of God's presence at Mount Sinai. Now, we're diving into the detailed instructions for building the Tabernacle, the place where God will dwell with his people. These chapters might read more like a construction blueprint rather than a meditation on spiritual insight. But I want to encourage you not to let the perceived dryness of these chapters cause you to skim over them. These are the moments when we must dig deeper, lean into God's Word, and allow it to shape our hearts. Yes, it may seem mundane at first, but trust me—God has something for us in these words if we approach them with open hearts.

You see, these chapters carry a deeper, more profound truth about the structure of worship itself. Throughout Christian history, there's been much debate about what worship should look like:

Should we worship with music, and if so, what kind? Pipe organs or electric guitars? Should it be in Latin, the language of tradition, or in the language of the people? These questions have divided congregations, denominations, and even entire movements. But when we look at the blueprint for the Tabernacle in Exodus 26, we see that the style of worship is secondary to something much deeper. What truly matters is the intentionality and the structure with which we approach God.

This passage lays out a powerful lesson for us. The Israelites had just been freed from slavery, and they were in the wilderness. They didn't have the wealth or resources of a settled people. They were nomads in the desert, not knowing what each new day would bring. But God was calling them to offer their best, to construct a sacred space where he could dwell among them. The materials for the Tabernacle weren't chosen out of convenience; they were carefully selected for their value and beauty. But God didn't ask the Israelites to seek out troves of treasures and rare materials. He simply asked them to give what they could. And that's the essence of worship that this passage calls us to understand: Worship is an act of intentionality, of planning, and of discipline. It requires us to offer what we have, even if what we have feels small in the face of God's greatness.

This is where the question of how we worship becomes secondary. It's not about the style, the instruments, the location, or the language; our hearts are truly what matter. The Tabernacle is a picture of worship that reflects both order and sacrifice. It was to be built with meticulous care and detail, reflecting the holiness of the God who would dwell there. There was nothing casual or haphazard about it. God was teaching the Israelites that when they came to worship, it should never be a thoughtless, unprepared act. Worship is not a box to check off or a simple routine to follow. It's a deliberate, heartfelt response to the God who frees us, who loves us, and who calls us into the divine presence.

I also want to point out another layer of this truth: Worship is an exercise in extravagant faith. The Israelites had so little in that moment, yet God was asking them to offer up what little they had for the sake of building something that would honor God. Those materials could have been used to bribe their way out of a dangerous situation or purchase goods necessary for survival. Instead, they invested them in God's presence. This is a key lesson for us. Worship is not only an act of discipline and order; it is also an act of faith and generosity. The Israelites were living in a desert, wandering without the comforts of home, but they gave what they had. Worship in its truest form calls us to give not out of abundance, but out of faith. It is an act of trust, believing that what we give to God—whether it's our time, our talents, our resources—will be used by him to accomplish his purposes.

Worship is a declaration that we trust God to provide for us, even when we feel we have little to offer.

And here's the truth for us today: Worship is about more than just the act itself; it's about what happens in our hearts. I have worshipped in the most beautiful cathedrals of Spain and in a dusty barn in the Arkansas Delta, with organs played by award-winning musicians, and with guitars played by seventh-graders who have had nine guitar lessons under their belt. God was praised not because of the details but because of the desire to show God how much he means to us. When we come before God with intentionality, structure, and generosity, we trust God will do something beautiful with our offering. We trust that God can take the little we have—whether that's our time, our energy, or our resources—and use it to build something far greater than we could ever imagine.

So, as we read through these chapters in Exodus, let's not rush through them. Let's sit with the lesson of the Tabernacle: Worship is a deliberate act, marked by intention, order, and generosity. It requires us to give, even when we feel we have little. But in doing so, we declare our trust in a God who has given us everything. May we approach worship with the same faith, discipline, and trust that the Israelites did when they built the Tabernacle. May we give with open hearts, believing that God will take our small offerings and transform them into something that reflects God's glory.

- How do you typically think about your time in worship? Have you ever thought about worship this way, as something that transforms your heart no matter how and where it happens?
- How could you be more intentional about praising God?

DAY 27

EXODUS 27

Key Verses: 27:20-21

Construction and maintenance are entirely different kinds of activities. It's one thing to lay a foundation and put up walls, but it's an entirely different thing to ensure that what has been built continues to function as it should. At the church I pastor, we have an entire team dedicated to the upkeep of our church building, people who work behind the scenes to make sure the lights stay on, the HVAC runs properly, and the place remains clean and welcoming for worship. Their work might not always be noticed, but without them, everything we do inside these walls would quickly fall into disorder.

The same principle applies to the Tabernacle in Exodus 27. After giving detailed instructions for its construction, God shifts the focus to something crucial: maintaining the lamp that is to burn continually inside. This isn't just a decorative touch or an afterthought; it's a command—one that requires ongoing commitment and effort. Someone has to be responsible for keeping the flame burning. Someone has to tend to it, to ensure it never goes out.

And this isn't just about a physical light. This lamp carries deep spiritual significance, reminding us of the role that light plays in our lives and in our faith. The command to keep the flame burning has layers of meaning, each one pointing us to a greater truth about who God is and what God calls us to do.

First, this light serves a practical purpose. Worship and sacrifices took place inside the Tabernacle, and people needed to see what they were doing. A place of worship without light would have been not only impractical but dangerous. This reminds us that God's presence isn't just theoretical; it's something that meets us in the real, tangible aspects of our lives. Just as the priests needed light to carry out their duties, we need the light of God to guide our steps, to illuminate the path before us, and to keep us from stumbling in the darkness.

Beyond its practical function, the lamp also carried a powerful symbolic meaning. Its constancy was a sign that the Tabernacle was a place of safety, reliability, and order in the midst of a chaotic and unpredictable world. Think about how darkness feels, how it can create uncertainty, fear, and vulnerability. Now, imagine walking into a place where the light never goes out, where there is always warmth, always clarity, always security. That's what the Tabernacle represented for the Israelites. It was a sanctuary, a safe and sacred place where God's presence provided stability in a world filled with threats and unknowns.

But perhaps most importantly, the lamp represented the very presence of God. Scripture tells us that in God there is no darkness at all. His presence is light itself—constant, unshakable, and illuminating. The Israelites were given the responsibility of maintaining this flame not because God needed light to see but because the burning lamp was a declaration: God is here. And through the work of the priests and the faithfulness of the people, that presence was assured.

Now, here's where this passage speaks directly to us. Just as the priests were tasked with keeping the flame burning in the Tabernacle, we are tasked with maintaining the flame of God's presence in our own lives. Faith isn't a one-time construction project; it's something that requires ongoing attention and care. We can't just build a relationship with God and then walk away, expecting it to sustain itself. The fire needs tending. The flame needs fuel. If we neglect it, it will dwindle, flicker, and eventually go out.

Each year for Christmas Eve, our church has the tradition of receiving the Bethlehem Peace Light. There is a grotto in the Church of the Nativity in Bethlehem where a flame has been continuously lit for over one thousand years. Each Christmas season, volunteers from around the world go and light candles and lanterns from that flame and then pass the light to homes and churches around the world to use in their Christmas Eve candlelight services. Keeping the flame burning through long drives and plane rides requires serious planning and care. It also brings a real sense of responsibility and pride to maintain the light and keep it burning at all times.

So how do we keep the flame of God's presence burning in our lives? The same way the priests did, through daily, intentional acts of faith. We feed the fire when we immerse ourselves in Scripture, allowing God's Word to light our path. We keep the lamp burning when we spend time in prayer, drawing near to the source of all light. We maintain the flame when we serve others, shining God's love into a world that desperately needs it.

This is our call. We are the light maintenance team. We have been entrusted with God's presence, and it's up to us to ensure that God's light doesn't fade in our hearts, our homes, and our communities. It's a daily responsibility, but it's also a daily privilege to be keepers of the flame, bearers of the light, and reminders to the world that God is still here.

So today, let's make it our mission to tend the fire. Let's commit to the work of maintaining the presence of God in our lives, not letting it grow dim through neglect or distraction. Let's be people who shine with the constancy of God's love, offering light to those who are searching for their way. The lamp in the Tabernacle was never meant to go out. Neither is the light of Christ in us.

- How can you better maintain the light of God in your life?
- How can you work to help others see the light that you are shining?

DAY 28

Exodus 28

Key Verses: 28:15-30

In this chapter of Exodus, we shift our focus from the construction of the Tabernacle itself to the garments worn by Aaron and his sons, those who will serve as priests before the Lord. While this may seem like a somewhat dull detour compared to the dramatic events earlier in the Exodus story, it carries deep significance. The way the priests were clothed was not an arbitrary decision; it was a reflection of the weight and holiness of their calling. These garments were not designed for comfort, fashion, or even practicality. They were designed with intention, crafted to communicate something powerful about the role of the priest.

God makes it clear that Aaron and his sons are not serving the people; they are serving God. Their role is unique. They stand in the sacred space between the holiness of God and the praise and repentance of the people. In a sense, they are a bridge, a connection point between heaven and earth, carrying the burdens of the people into the presence of God. And because of this, every aspect of their appearance is meant to reflect the gravity of their role. Do you see your pastor or priest living into the same role today? I don't often think of myself in this way, so this shift in perspective is interesting to me.

One of the most striking pieces of the priestly attire is the breastplate. It is described with extreme detail here in Exodus and again in Leviticus 8:6-9. Even among the extravagant designs of the Tabernacle, the breastplate stands out. Its construction is intricate, its materials are costly, and its symbolism is profound. The people of Israel were called to contribute the best of what they had: gold, fine linen, and twelve precious stones, each representing one of the twelve tribes. Every color, every gem, every stitch was intentional. This was not a simple accessory; it was a declaration of identity, a visible sign that the priest carried the entire nation with him into the presence of God.

The stones listed on the breastplate are particularly interesting. They are rare and obscure, appearing only three other times in Scripture. One passage references the arrogance of a foreign nation known for its wealth. Another speaks of the value of wisdom in the book of Job. The final reference describes the beauty of a cherished wife. Each time, these stones are used to indicate something beyond the ordinary, something of extreme worth and loveliness, something to take pride in. And here, they are placed upon Aaron as he steps into his role as intercessor for the people.

Why would God command such an extravagant display? Why not something simpler, something more practical? Because God understands human nature. God knows that what we wear often shapes how we carry ourselves.

I have a good friend who is a high-ranking officer in the United States Air Force, but I had never seen her in her official military dress uniform. I had only seen her as a wife, mother, friend, and church member. I will never forget the first time I saw her in her dress blues, and my behavior and demeanor around her changed. Her official appearance shifted my perception of her, even though her countenance and attitude hadn't changed at all. You have likely experienced this seeing a police officer in uniform or a medical professional in scrubs, perhaps especially if that person was known to you first as a personal friend or relative. The uniform makes a difference in how we think about someone and what we believe they are capable of achieving. And the priestly garments were meant to do just that, to remind Aaron of the weight of his calling and to remind the people of the holiness of God.

While we don't wear priestly garments today, this passage does speak to something important about how we approach God. We often talk about the beauty of being able to come to God "just as we are," and that is absolutely true. God welcomes us with open arms, whether we are put together or falling apart. But at the same time, I wonder if we sometimes approach God too casually, forgetting the immense privilege of standing in God's presence.

The issue isn't about what we wear but about the posture of our hearts. Do we come before God with a sense of awe, or do we rush into prayer without a second thought? Do we approach the throne of grace with reverence, or do we treat it as just another item on our to-do list? The priests were required to prepare themselves before entering God's presence, and while our preparation looks different today, the principle remains: We should never take for granted the holiness of the one we are speaking to.

This doesn't mean we should be afraid to approach God. In fact, because of Jesus we have been given the great gift of approaching God as a loving father. But boldness does not mean carelessness. Boldness and reverence can exist together. When we recognize that we are speaking to the creator of the universe, the one who holds all things together, it actually deepens our prayers. It reminds us that we are not just tossing words into the air, hoping for something to stick. We are speaking to the Almighty, the one who can move mountains, heal wounds, and transform lives.

So today, let's take a moment to reflect on how we approach God. Let's not be casual in our prayers, but intentional. Let's not treat time with God as an afterthought, but as a sacred opportunity. And let's remember that when we bow in prayer, we are standing in the presence of the king of all creation. May that truth give us both humility and confidence as we seek God today.

- How can you more humbly and reverently approach God in prayer?
- How would your prayer life change if you fully acknowledged the power of God each time you prayed?

DAY 29

Exodus 29

Key Verses: 29:38-42

As we journey deeper into Exodus, we come across the instructions for the daily offering, a rhythm of worship that was to take place morning and evening. Every single day, without fail, a lamb was to be sacrificed in the morning and another in the evening. This wasn't just about the act of sacrifice itself; it was about the formation of a holy community. Through these offerings, the Israelites were reminded daily of their dependence on God, their need for atonement, and their call to holiness. This is where holiness is created—not in isolation but within the life of a faithful community. It was through these daily, repeated acts of devotion that the people were shaped into who God was calling them to be. The sacrifices were not random; they were a structured and intentional way to maintain a relationship with a holy God.

Within this passage, we also see a distinction between the Tabernacle and the tent of meeting. While both are sacred spaces, they serve different purposes. The Tabernacle is where God dwells; it is God's established place of presence among the people. But the tent of meeting is where God comes for specific engagements, moments of divine encounter. And what brings God to these meetings? Not elaborate speeches, not intellectual debates, but the offering of daily essentials, bulls, lambs, rams, flour, and wafers. In other words, God meets the people in the very fabric of their existence, in the things that sustain their daily lives.

This is a powerful truth for us today. Holiness is not just about what we believe. It is about what we do. It is not formed in our minds alone but in the practices of our daily lives. The Israelites were not made holy by simply thinking the right thoughts or agreeing with the right doctrines; they became holy by doing the right things in the right ways. Their faith was embodied in their actions, in their discipline, in their commitment to offering up their very sustenance to God.

John Wesley, the founder of Methodism, would later emphasize this same idea. He believed that faith was not merely a set of beliefs but a way of life. He called it "practical divinity," a faith that is lived out through acts of service, devotion, and love. According to Wesley, holiness is not something we achieve by accident but rather something we cultivate through intentional practices: serving others, proclaiming the good news, immersing ourselves in Scripture, and developing a deep life of prayer. It is in the daily rhythms of faithfulness that we are transformed.

This challenges us to think about our own spiritual practices. Are we only seeking God in extraordinary moments, or are we allowing his presence to shape our everyday lives? Do we recognize that holiness is cultivated in the small, consistent acts of faith, morning prayers, moments of gratitude, service to others, generosity, and devotion? I have found that God often grabs our attention and begins a relationship with us through some miraculous moment of rescue or redemption, but the real meat of the relationship comes in the long and steady decisions of discipleship. It reminds me of my love for my wife. Initially, our love was born out of exciting conversations, with sparks of chemistry flying all around, but the depth of our love grew in the ordinary days of raising children, caring for parents, and growing up together. It was our decision to continue to choose each other in those moments that allowed our connection to thrive. Our connection to God is the same.

God's call to holiness and discipleship is not an abstract concept; it is deeply practical. It is found in how we live, how we treat others, how we worship, and how we trust God with our daily needs. The Israelites were asked to give from their sustenance, to return to God what had been provided to them. We, too, are invited to offer our time, our energy, our resources, and our very lives as acts of worship. So today, let's take inventory of our own daily offerings. What are we giving to God? Are we carving out time for him, or is he an afterthought in the busyness of our schedules? Are we practicing our faith in tangible ways, or do we simply believe the right things without putting them into action? Let's commit to living out our faith, knowing that holiness is not just something we think about. It is something we do.

- How are you practicing your faith this week? What actions could you pick up that would help you be more holy?
- How do you think about the idea of obedience to God? Do you find it freeing? Constraining? Why?

DAY 30

Exodus 30

Key Verses: Exodus 30:11-16

I love the way God orders the Israelites, the way God orchestrates their culture and way of life with purpose and intentionality. Nothing is left to chance, every detail, from the instruments of worship to the way the people sustain the Tabernacle, is laid out and laden with meaning. In today's key verses, we see an often-overlooked instruction: the command for what is called in verse 16 the "atonement money."

At first glance, this may seem like just a practical solution for maintaining the Tabernacle. After all, running a place of worship requires resources. But as with all of God's commands, this is about more than just logistics. This command speaks directly to the heart of community, responsibility, and spiritual investment.

God instructs Moses to take a census, registering all those who belong to the community of the redeemed. This census isn't just a headcount. It's more important: It's a declaration of identity. To be counted is to belong. And with belonging comes responsibility. Every adult is required to give a half shekel to support the work of the Tabernacle. The amount isn't dependent on wealth, status, or personal resources. It is the same for everyone, rich or poor. This was a gift that united the people, a tangible expression of their shared faith and commitment.

This is a powerful concept. In most offerings, people give according to what they have. Some can give more, others less, and generosity is measured in proportion to one's means. But this specific offering was different. It wasn't about wealth; it was about unity. Every person had the same responsibility because every person belonged equally to the people of God. The Tabernacle wasn't just for the wealthy or the elite. It was for everyone. And if it was for everyone, then everyone had a role to play in sustaining it.

I love this idea of universal investment in the worshipping body. Later, God will establish the tithe, giving ten percent of one's earnings, as an act of worship and trust. That principle is vital. But there is something uniquely powerful about a simple, small offering that every person gives, regardless of their situation. It's a reminder that faith is not just personal but communal. Worship isn't just something we receive; it's something we participate in. We are able to give because of the abundant way that God has given to us.

And this truth carries forward to us today. The church, the body of Christ, should not be sustained by the generosity of just a few. It flourishes when every believer is committed, invested, and engaged. Just like in the days of the Israelites, our mission and ministry require the faithfulness of the entire community. Some are able to give more financially; others have more time to serve; and still others bring gifts of leadership, prayer, or hospitality. But all of us, every single one of us, have a role to play.

I think of this whenever I see the credits roll at the end of a movie. Often we think that the movie hinges on the lead actors or the director, but the key grips and best boys are just as critical to making a great film. A movie set, like a church, needs everyone to be fully invested and working for the success of the whole.

So today, let's reflect on our own investment in God's work. Are we merely attending, or are we actively participating? Do we see ourselves as spectators or as contributors? What simple, consistent gift can we offer—whether of our time, our resources, or our talents—to sustain and strengthen the work of God's church? Let us be people who don't just belong in name but in action. May we each bring our offering, whatever it may be, and declare with our lives that we are fully invested in the kingdom of God.

- How can you use this chapter from Exodus or the reflections on it here to teach your children and grandchildren about the importance of committed generosity to God and the church?
- Can you think of a way to make a small gift to your church that would benefit its ministries?

DAY 31

Exodus 31

Key Verses: Exodus 31:1-11

In these verses, God offers a moment of reassurance to Moses, who must have been feeling an immense weight of responsibility pressing down on him. Imagine standing in his shoes: He has just received the most intricate and detailed instructions on building the Tabernacle, a dwelling place for God. Every specification must be followed precisely. But then the inevitable question arises: Who is going to do all of this work? Who among these wandering former slaves has the skill to transform wood, gold, and fabric into a structure worthy of God's presence? It must have been overwhelming. But as always, God provides.

God's answer comes in the form of two artisans: Bezalel and Oholiab. These two men, though virtually unknown outside of these passages, are chosen for the task ahead. Their names do not carry the same weight in biblical history as Moses or Aaron, but their role is similarly vital. They are not just competent craftsmen; they are filled with the Spirit of God, endowed with wisdom, understanding, and skill in all forms of artistry. I find it interesting that these men are described as being filled with the Spirit, as that language reminds us so much of what happens at Pentecost. There we see other ordinary men and women filled with the Holy Spirit and tasked with building the church of Jesus. Here, two men are divinely equipped to oversee and execute the construction of the Tabernacle, ensuring that every detail aligns with God's plan.

There's a powerful lesson here. As the saying goes, "God doesn't call the qualified; he qualifies the called." But perhaps it's more accurate to say that God calls people with the right gifts for a particular task, and then, through the power of the Holy Spirit, God strengthens, inspires, and equips them further. Bezalel and Oholiab have natural talent, but their ability to transform raw materials into something sacred was a result of divine empowerment.

This passage also reveals something profound about the relationship between God and humanity. In Genesis, God created the world, a home for humankind, through God's own power. Now, in Exodus, he invites humanity to create a home for him. The construction of the Tabernacle is not simply a human project; it is a Spirit-led endeavor, a reflection of God's creative nature within us. Just as God spoke the world into existence, God now speaks through people to craft a space for the divine presence.

This truth extends far beyond Bezalel and Oholiab. God continues to call and equip people today for his ongoing work.

God has given each of us gifts and talents that can be used to build the Kingdom. Perhaps you have a heart for teaching, a talent for building, a knack for mentoring, or an eye for artistry. Maybe you're gifted in hospitality, music, or administration. Whatever your abilities, they are not accidental; they are purposeful, given by God to be used for his glory.

If God is still in the business of calling and equipping God's people, are we willing to listen and respond? Bezalel and Oholiab could have doubted their ability or resisted the call, but instead, they stepped forward in obedience. What might God be calling you to build, create, or lead? How is the Holy Spirit equipping you for the work ahead? You don't have to be a pastor or a theologian to do God's work. You just have to be willing. Take time today to reflect on the gifts God has placed within you. How can you use them to serve the church, strengthen your community, and glorify God? God is still calling his people to create, to build, and to minister. May we, like Bezalel and Oholiab, answer that call with faithful and willing hearts.

- What are your skills and strengths? Be honest with yourself and don't downplay your experience.
- How could you use those gifts to glorify God, either through the church or on your own in the world?

DAY 32

Exodus 32

Key Verses: 32:1-14

Forty days. That's all it took. Forty days without Moses, and the Israelites lost their faith completely. After witnessing God fighting for them through the plagues, the parting of the Red Sea, manna from heaven, and the very presence of God in the thunder and fire on Mount Sinai, forty days was all it took for them to turn away.

Lent is forty days for a reason. It mirrors Jesus's time of fasting in the wilderness, and it also echoes this moment in Exodus. The Israelites were being tested, just as we are. They had been freed from Egypt, but Egypt was still inside them. They had seen God's power, but their hearts had not yet learned to trust God. How often are we the same? We commit to following God, but when we don't see immediate results, we start looking for something, anything, else to fill the void. How quick am I to give God my heart in worship on Sunday but look to my own arrogance or some vice on Thursday, when the going gets tough?

This golden calf moment is one of the most devastating in Israel's history. It is their fall, just as Adam and Eve's sin was humanity's first rebellion in Eden. It's not just a moment of doubt, it's a full rejection of the covenant they made with God. They don't just make an idol; they throw a wild, drunken festival around it. Their worship turns into revelry, chaos, and the outright breakdown of everything God hoped they could become. They are no longer the people God called them to be, for they have become lost in their own selfishness and impatience.

And yet, in the middle of this disaster, we see the power of an intercessor. Moses stands in the gap between the people and God. God is heartbroken, righteously angry, and ready to wipe them out. He tells Moses, "Let me alone so that my wrath may burn hot against them" (verse 10). But Moses doesn't back away. He doesn't take God's offer to start over with him alone. Instead, he pleads for mercy. He reminds God of the promises, of God's faithfulness and reputation among the nations. And, incredibly, God relents.

This is what true leadership looks like. Moses doesn't excuse the people's sin. He will confront them, hold them accountable, and lead them to repentance. But he also won't let them be abandoned. He fights for them, even when they don't deserve it. Can you imagine being someone's defense attorney only to then become the one carrying out their punishment? Moses's job here is beyond difficult, but because of his faithful connection to God, he is able to lead the people with integrity and honesty.

So, how does this speak to us today? The story reminds us that we need to deeply examine our own hearts. Where have we turned to our own golden calves in our impatience? Have we made idols out of success, relationships, or comfort? Have we allowed our worship to become about what we want rather than who God is? And just as importantly, are we willing to be intercessors for others? Are we willing to stand in the gap, to pray for those who have wandered, to plead with God on their behalf?

Moses foreshadows Jesus in this moment. Just as Moses interceded for the people, Jesus intercedes for us. When we fail, when we are faithless, Jesus is faithful. He does not abandon us, even when we deserve it. This is the grace of God: that even when we turn away, God still calls us back.

As we continue to journey through these forty days, let us be mindful of our own tendency to stray. Let us seek God with patient hearts, trusting that God's timing is perfect. And let us be people of intercession—standing in the gap for others, as Christ does for us.

- It only took forty days for the rescued slaves to seek another god. How are we like the Israelites? What do we worship when we feel abandoned? How can we seek to be different?
- How can you be more like Moses, obedient to God even when obedience is difficult?

DAY 33

Exodus 33

Key Verses: 33:17-23

At the end of chapter 32, Israel is in acute crisis. Chapter 33 is the story of how they are going to move forward with God. Their next steps are crucial because the people of Israel were nothing before the Exodus, and their identity and status in the world after it is based on their covenant with God. A fracture in the covenant is also a fracture in what holds them together and sets them apart. The question boils down to God's presence. Will God still dwell with them? Will that Tabernacle be needed after all?

Again, we see Moses standing in the gap between God and Israel, working to repair the damage. Moses is relentless with God, ensuring that God intends to keep the promise of leading these people into a bountiful land, being with them always. Moses's relationship with God is one of the most fleshed out and intimate that we see in the entire Bible, and in a moment of full courage, he asks to see the very core of God, the fullness of God's presence. God's response to this request is four powerful affirmations and one massive negative at the end. The four affirmations of Exodus 33:19, along with their explanations, are as follows:

1. "I will make all my goodness pass before you." These are the gifts of God's presence and blessing. Ultimate relief must have washed over Moses in this moment. God will not abandon them.
2. "(I) will proclaim before you the name, 'the Lord.'" This is about the full disclosure of God's character. This is a promise of real intimacy. God is divulging his heart to Moses. What a beautiful moment between God and God's people.
3. "I will be gracious to whom I will be gracious." God's generosity will be with the people. In a moment when God has every right to stop being so kind, so good, so loving, God doubles down on the promise to love and care for them.
4. "I will show mercy on whom I show mercy." At the heart of God's character is forgiveness, a willingness to not just overlook the sins of the people but to truly absolve them and move on in a new way.

Directly after offering these affirmations, God says, "You cannot see my face, for no one shall see me and live" (v. 20) but offers Moses some temporary protection so that he may glimpse

God's back. There have been strains and trials for God and Moses's relationship, but the intimacy that is shown throughout this chapter shows that there is clearly also redemption and repair. Thus, forgiveness begins to take shape for the people of God.

I think of this passage often when people say that the God of the Old Testament was angry and vengeful. That is certainly not the heart and character of God that we see here. I am quick to point to this story to highlight the love and grace on display here and God's abiding desire to love and save his people. The God who reveals himself to Moses is the God who will reveal himself to us all in Jesus. God's saving work started with Adam and Eve and will not end until the Kingdom comes in fullness and truth.

- Does this reading change the way you think about God's character in the Old Testament?
- How can you boldly approach God like Moses did, and ask to see and hear God more clearly?

DAY 34

Exodus 34

Key Verses: 34:6-7

Today is all about the reconciliation and forgiveness that comes only through the hands of God. Our key verses today are God's own self-disclosure about his very nature. The name of God being uttered here reminds us of the story of Moses and the burning bush, when God says "I am who I am" in response to being asked about the divine name.

In this passage, God chooses to remain as sovereign over the people of God. And important things about God's nature are revealed in two movements.

First, Yahweh is wondrously generous and forgiving, and only Yahweh's generosity and forgiveness could restore Israel. Seven terms are used to make this assertion, and they form the Old Testament's core vocabulary for describing God's character. Let's walk through them together.

- *Merciful*. The word in Hebrew is *rahum*, which is closely connected to the noun *rehem*, which means "womb." It connotes the love of a mother for her child.

Here we reflect on the sacrificial love of our mothers and/or other important women in our lives who gave so much so we might have and succeed in life.

- *Gracious.* This is about unmerited favor, completely gratuitous positive inclination. Read that description again. Can you imagine feeling that way toward anyone? Seeing no negative components in them, loving them in the most generous way. It is almost too much to comprehend.
- *Slow to anger.* In Hebrew, the words here literally mean "long nosed." Taken literally, God's anger was a fire breathing out of God's nose, and a longer nostril would give it time to cool down. Such a vivid image speaks to God's desire to love instead of punish.
- *Abounding in steadfast love.* This is a play on the word *hesed*, which is a kind of lovingkindness. "Abounding" here speaks to the fact that God will hold *hesed* for the people and will be willing to put up with a great deal from them while continuing to love them. We see *hesed* throughout the Old Testament, from Abraham and Rebekah, Ruth and Boaz, and from Jonathan for David. God gives us this quality to share with others.
- *Faithfulness.* A close synonym to *hesed*, this word (*emet*) speaks to God's complete reliability. The phrase *hesed we emet* occurs frequently and is often echoed

in the New Testament to describe Christ. Love and faithfulness are the heart of God.

- *Keeping steadfast love. Hesed* will be passed down for generations. God is in this for the long haul. This is not a contract of convenience but a covenant of love.
- *Forgiving.* The Hebrew word is *nasa*, which literally means "to lift." This is about lifting the burden of covenant violation off the sinner's back. God is willing to bear the burden we cannot bear on our own. Christ bears the weight of our sins on the cross, and through his death and resurrection, we are able to stand again.

Taken together, these qualities speak to the fact that God is deeply committed to sustaining a covenant with Israel. It is crucial that we see how powerful it is that this incredible moment of God's self-disclosure happens not in a time of victory but when God is deeply offended and the people are in jeopardy.

Now, we need to discuss the other side of the coin. God also responds with sovereign ferocity to affront. Two more stern terms describing God's character are found here, in contradistinction to the seven positive ones:

- *God will not acquit.* While God is forgiving, God does not overlook violations of the covenant. God still cares what we do. If we really consider this point, it makes God more loving. God isn't some absentee parent who lets us do whatever we want, even if it means we are doing damage to ourselves and others. Our behavior matters deeply to God, and we will be held accountable.

- *God will visit.* God will not be mocked and grace is not cheap. The people's sinfulness will be forgiven, but they will feel the result of their decision making. We will face the ramifications of our actions.

What is interesting about this self-revelation of God is that every characteristic is bound by relationship. For example, God isn't describing divine omnipotence or omniscience, which are qualities that we ascribe to God in all times and places, even before and apart from the creation of the universe. Rather, the characteristics listed in Exodus 34 are all about how God stands specifically in relationship to Israel. In other words, God's self-definition is in part based on the desire to be in a relationship with us. Yes, God is all-powerful. Of course, God is all-knowing by nature. Yet God chooses to be defined in social terms that will help lead us into a deeper connection with him. For that we should be deeply grateful.

- Are any of the characteristics above surprising to you? Which was the most meaningful for you? Which connects most to your life of faith?
- How do you feel knowing that God's chosen self-definition includes a desire to be in a relationship with you and the rest of humanity?

DAY 35

Exodus 35

Key Verses: 35:20-29

It is time for the actual construction of the Tabernacle, and this is going to require the people of God to give of themselves. There are two key aspects in this report of unprecedented generosity. Behind this financial transaction lies an intense religious motivation, with hearts stirring and spirits willing. This is worship, not business. This paints a picture of a community so convinced of the strength of its covenant and the divine truth behind its liberation that it is willing to act with abandon.

I have experienced this on mission trips in my home state of Arkansas, as church groups from around the state would gather together, worship as one body, and then spring forth into action to love our neighbors and serve those in need. The work of building wheelchair ramps and repairing homes sprang forth as an extension of worship. We weren't singing or reading Scripture or listening to sermons, but we were praising God with the swinging of hammers and buzzing of saws.

The second pervasive feature here is the word "all." There is participation from everyone, both men and women, leaders and laypeople, those who have goods and those who have skill, each giving according to their possessions and abilities. This suggests an image of a community alive, stirred, and energized to act in ways that extend beyond what they thought possible. This is a once-in-a-lifetime effort for a once-in-a-lifetime purpose.

But how do the people get so energized here?

- There is promise and expectation that this offering will provide a Tabernacle in which God will actually dwell with them. God will not just visit but *be* with them. They have experienced God's power and forgiveness. They have seen the very heart of God, and they are exhilarated at the opportunity to be with God always.
- They have come face to face with forgiveness and been given a second chance. That is a powerful motivator to get things right. Notice that for the building of the calf they just gave earrings, but for this they give jewelry of every kind. They have learned their lesson and are doing things the right way.
- The Israelites have learned that God is wildly generous and gives abundantly. As a result, they have learned

that their sacrifices are actually a gift they can offer back to God. They are giving out of their abundance, learning it is better to give than receive. They are no longer the destitute slaves without anything to offer; they are a people of the Most High God.

- God's Tabernacle is a chance for them to have a "home" and no longer be a people on the run. If home is where the heart is, their hearts will rest in God's presence, which dwells in the Tabernacle.

The real question is how we can tap into that kind of motivation, because everything that is true for the Israelites is also true for us. God has promised to be with us through the Holy Spirit. We have been granted forgiveness from our sinfulness. We have been blessed by God abundantly, and we have a home in Christ. Let us respond as our ancestors did, giving all we have to the glory of God.

- How are you giving of yourself to build God's kingdom today, in the way the Israelites built the Tabernacle long ago?
- When were you most excited and energized about God's presence in your life? Can you recapture that exuberance? How?

DAY 36

Exodus 36

Key Verses: 36:3-7

If you have been around the church for long, you know the typical pattern of pastors leading stewardship campaigns in the month of October. This tradition stems from our agrarian past, aligning a season of generosity with the season of the harvest. It makes sense, doesn't it? Harvest time is when farmers see the fruits of their labor, a tangible reminder of God's provision.

But I will never forget a conversation I had with a retired pastor who took a very different approach. He told me that he always started his stewardship campaigns the Sunday following Easter. His reasoning? People would be more generous when they had just celebrated the salvation from their sins found in the Cross and Resurrection. He didn't share whether that approach actually led to larger offerings, but his working theory stuck with me. If he had rooted that theory in our passage today, I might have believed him wholeheartedly.

Here, we find a truly remarkable moment in the history of God's people. The artisans working on the Tabernacle are overwhelmed not by the demands of their labor but by the sheer volume of offerings brought to them. Morning after morning, the people come with their gifts, freely and joyfully giving what they have to ensure that God's dwelling place is built with excellence. Eventually, the workmen report to Moses that they have more than enough material. Imagine that, a moment so overflowing with generosity that Moses has to command the people to *stop* giving! This is a moment of unrestrained devotion, an outpouring of gratitude for all that God has done.

What makes this so powerful is that the people's generosity is not calculated or hesitant. They are not giving out of obligation, nor are they measuring their gifts to make sure they still have plenty left for themselves. Their giving is extravagant, an expression of their overwhelming gratitude for God's presence, provision, and faithfulness. They aren't just donating resources; they are responding to God's mercy and grace with open hearts and willing spirits.

This passage forces us to ask an important question: Are we responding to God in the same way? We have received everything the Israelites did and more. We have the fullness of God's presence through the Holy Spirit. We have the promise of salvation through Christ. We have seen the faithfulness of God in our own lives, time and time again. And yet, do we give with the same joy, the same reckless generosity? Or do we simply offer what is left over after we've taken care of everything else?

I pray that we would model our giving after the people of Israel in this passage—not as a duty but as an act of joyful, extravagant devotion. May our generosity be a reflection of the generosity God has already shown to us.

- Would it be difficult to give more of your time, energy, and finances to God? What strains might this create, and what benefits and blessings would you see?
- The Israelites' offering is a response to God's generosity. How can you cultivate that same kind of thoughtfulness about what God has done for you?

DAY 37

Exodus 37

Key Verses: 37:15-16

Almost two weeks ago, I warned you about a few days of reading that were going to be pretty dry compared to other parts of Exodus. Well, here we are. But if there is anything we have learned so far, it is that God can and will reveal vital meaning and value even in the most seemingly mundane passages. Scripture reminds us time and again that faithfulness is not just found in the grand, miraculous moments but in the steady, daily obedience to God's call.

The construction of the Tabernacle and all the necessary items for its operation is now underway. This entire account is filled with specific instructions and meticulous details, reinforcing the sacredness of what is being built. Every item serves a purpose, and every detail reflects God's intentionality. But as we read through this chapter, an important phrase appears repeatedly: "He made."

This simple phrase carries a powerful message. The "he" refers to Bezalel, the artisan appointed by God to lead the construction efforts. Over and over, the passage repeats, "He made." It may seem redundant, but it underscores an essential truth: Faithfulness requires sustained, steady obedience that all moves in the same direction. The work of building the Tabernacle wasn't completed by a single miraculous event. It was the result of repeated, disciplined effort, day in and day out, faithfully following God's instructions.

Isn't that a beautiful and practical definition of faith? A lifelong journey of obedience, choosing to live like Christ each day, in small and consistent ways. Faithfulness is not just or even really about believing the right things or reciting the right prayers. It is about the steady, often unseen work of following God. It is about waking up each morning and choosing to serve, to love, and to grow. It is about honoring God not just in the extraordinary moments but in the ordinary ones as well.

Imagine if we personalized this passage. Instead of the phrase "he made" referring to the construction of sacred furniture, what if it reflected the way we live out our faith? What if our daily acts of obedience were recorded in this way?

- He made peace with someone he held a grudge against.
- She made time to check on a struggling friend.
- He made an intentional effort to pray more deeply.
- She made space in her life to serve the church.
- He made an impact on someone by offering kindness.
- She made a habit of starting her day with Scripture.

These are the acts of obedience that build a life of faithfulness. These are the steady, quiet, persistent actions that draw us closer to God. Just as Bezalel followed God's instructions in constructing the Tabernacle, we, too, are called to build a life of faith, one act of obedience at a time.

It is easy to grow weary in faithfulness. Some days, obedience feels exciting and full of purpose, while others, it feels tedious or even seems to go unnoticed. But Scripture reminds us that our faithfulness, no matter how small, matters deeply to God. Galatians 6:9 encourages us: "Let us not grow weary in doing what is right, for we will reap at harvest time, if we do not give up."

God will use our hands to do great things when we offer them as tools for God's kingdom. He will take our simple, daily acts of obedience and weave them into something sacred, something lasting, something that reveals God's presence to the world.

So today, let us embrace the call to steady, faithful obedience. Let us commit to the "he made" moments in our own lives, knowing that in each act of love, service, and worship, we are building something holy—a life that reflects the goodness and glory of God. May we be faithful in the work, trusting that God is using every small act of obedience for building up the Kingdom.

- Do you ever get tired of the long work of obedience? How do you find strength in those moments?
- What will you make today for God?

DAY 38

Exodus 38

Key Verses: 38:21-31

I love it when Scripture mirrors real life. We often think that the Bible is just filled with fantastical stories of men being swallowed by whales and miraculous healings. But in our key verses today, we get the most practical of realities: accounting.

Our key verses present the final audit of the finances, divided into two parts. First, we see the three responsible officers who are signatories to the final contract. Then we see a report on the actual expenditure of the funds. So, while the community may have given extravagantly, those responsible for the project must be precise to cover the actual costs and give an account of their management. This passage also makes me thankful for the accountants in my life who take care of the financial details and make sure everything is squared away.

What I find so powerful about this is that God cares about the details of our lives and wants us to be good stewards of all that we have and give. That goes for all of us, from churches and nonprofits to businesses and our households. God desires us to use our resources wisely to best care for our families and organizations as well as the kingdom of God. We may not always think of accounting as a holy task, but maybe we should, as God clearly cares about it.

The transparency shown in Exodus 38 teaches us that generosity and stewardship must go hand in hand. The Israelites had given freely and sacrificially for the construction of the Tabernacle, but the leaders did not take that generosity lightly. Every contribution was accounted for; every resource tracked; and every piece of gold, silver, and bronze was put to use as intended. This level of care and diligence in these matters sets an example for us in our own lives. Whether we are overseeing church funds, managing household budgets, or donating to charities, we should be intentional and responsible with what has been entrusted to us.

This passage also highlights the importance of accountability in leadership. The work of building the Tabernacle was not a solo effort. Bezalel and Oholiab had been appointed to oversee the craftsmanship, but they were also accountable to others. Ithamar, a priestly figure, was responsible for auditing and recording the materials used. This structure ensured that resources were not wasted, mismanaged, or otherwise used inappropriately. It serves as a model for us in positions of leadership, whether in the church, workplace, or community, to operate with integrity and transparency.

When we practice faithful stewardship, we reflect God's order and wisdom in our daily lives. Stewardship is not just about money; it is about managing all that God has given us, our time, talents, and treasures, for God's glory. The Israelites were not just building a structure; they were creating a space where God's presence would dwell among them. In the same way, when we use our resources wisely, we create opportunities for God's work to be done in our lives and in the world around us.

Perhaps we should start viewing our financial decisions as an act of worship. Every budget we create, every offering we give, every resource we steward with integrity can be a reflection of our faithfulness to God. Just as the Israelites honored God by giving generously and managing their gifts wisely, we, too, can honor God by being faithful stewards of what God has entrusted to us.

So today, let's take a moment to reflect on how we manage what God has given us. Are we generous in our giving? Are we diligent in our stewardship? Are we operating with integrity and transparency in our financial decisions? If God finds accounting worthy of mention in Scripture, perhaps we should find it worthy of our attention as well. May we be people who give freely and steward wisely, knowing that every resource we manage is an opportunity to glorify God.

- How can you be a better holy accountant of how you use what God has given you?
- If you were to do a holy audit on your time, energy, and resources, what areas might need some improvement? Where could you do more for God's kingdom?

DAY 39

Exodus 39

Key Verses: 39:32-43

Complete. It's a powerful word, isn't it? Concluded, done, over. The Tabernacle, and all of the work and faithfulness that went into its construction, is "was finished" (v. 32). The Hebrew word here can also mean "achieved" or "fulfilled." I like those definitions better. This is a beautiful moment between God and the Israelite people. They are still wandering in the wilderness, yet they have created a home for God to dwell with them. They are a people loved by the God of all creation, who will be with them wherever they go. Just a few months earlier, though, they were a destitute people trapped in slavery. The road to this stop was full of ups and downs, and yet they made it. And when they did, Moses's response was to bless them, give thanks for them, and rejoice in this beautiful moment.

The completion of the Tabernacle is not just an achievement in craftsmanship; it is an achievement in faith. The people followed God's instructions, gave generously, and worked diligently, and now they stand before a sacred space where God's presence will dwell among them. Imagine the sense of accomplishment and awe they must have felt. It wasn't just about building something; it was about obedience, devotion, and trust in God's guidance.

There's something deeply human about this moment. We, too, long for completion: for projects finished, goals met, and journeys fulfilled. But we also recognize that true fulfillment comes not just from the work of our hands but from the faithfulness of our hearts as well. The Israelites completed their task, but their journey with God was far from over. Just as they built a dwelling place for God in the wilderness, we are called to make space for God in our hearts and lives every day, no matter where we are on our own trek through the wilderness.

As our journey through Exodus and Lent draws to a close, I hope you have been able to see yourself in the people of God. For you were once a slave to sin and death, then saved by the God of all creation and tasked with the responsibility to build God's kingdom. While our work is not complete, this season of Lent is almost fulfilled, and we will celebrate together the risen Christ very soon. But today is Good Friday, and before we can celebrate, we must remember the agony our savior endured for our sake and give thanks.

The cross stands as a reminder that Jesus, too, achieved what he was sent to do. His work was finished but not in the sense of being over—it was fulfilled. He bore our sin, suffered our punishment, and opened the way for us to dwell eternally with God. And just as Moses blessed the people after their faithful work, Jesus's final act was one of blessing: a sacrifice that would bring eternal life to all who believe.

So, take a few moments today, friends, and remember the debt that Christ paid for you and just how much it cost. Reflect on the price of grace. Repent of your sins, and be thankful for a God who rescues. May we, like the Israelites, build something meaningful with our lives—spaces where God's presence is welcomed, honored, and cherished. And may we walk into the celebration of Easter knowing that the work of salvation has been fulfilled, once and for all.

- Reflect on the completion of the Tabernacle. Does using the word "achieve" or "fulfill" change your understanding of the Israelites' work on the Tabernacle? How might this apply to your own spiritual journey?
- Moses responds to the completed work with blessing and gratitude. How can we cultivate a similar attitude of thanksgiving in our own faith communities and personal lives?
- On this Good Friday, how can remembering Christ's suffering deepen your appreciation for God's presence in your life?

DAY 40

Exodus 40

Key Verses: 40:34-38

Friends, I hope your Lenten journey has been one of profound faith development. As we come to the end of this forty-day reflection, I pray that God has used the story of the Israelites and their relationship with him to deepen your life of faith and to draw you into a closer and more intimate walk with God. It has been a privilege to be on this path with you, sharing in the highs and lows of the Israelites' journey and reflecting on how their story mirrors our own.

As we reach the conclusion of our study, I am reminded of the Israelites' final days in the wilderness. The tabernacle was finally completed, and God's presence came to dwell among them in a powerful way. Exodus 40:34-38 describes how the cloud of the Lord's presence covered the tabernacle by day and the pillar of fire guided them by night. It was a tangible sign that God was with them, leading them, guiding them toward the Promised Land from the beginning of the journey to this very moment.

But even as the Israelites' journey seemed to reach a conclusion, it was really only the beginning. God's work was not done; God still had plans for them. The cloud and fire would continue to lead them forward, step by step, as they moved toward the fulfillment of God's promises. And just as it wasn't the end for the Israelites, it isn't the end for us. God has a purpose and plan for each of us, and our journey with God continues beyond these forty days.

As you reflect on the journey we've walked together during this season of Lent, I encourage you to look ahead. Just as God led the Israelites with the cloud and fire, God still leads us today, calls us to build the Kingdom and to live faithfully in the world he has called us to, and to be his hands and feet. The promise of God's presence remains with us, and thus, we are never alone.

In the days ahead, let us keep our eyes on the horizon, looking for the ways God is leading us—through the quiet whisper of the Holy Spirit, through the guidance of Scripture, and through the community of believers God has placed around us. The end of this season of Lent is not the end of the journey; it's simply a moment to pause, reflect, and prepare for the road ahead.

You will continue to be in my prayers, friends, as we walk together, side by side, into the future God has prepared for us. I hope you will pray for me as well. Let us journey on, with hearts full of faith and eyes open to where God is leading next.

- How have you experienced God's guidance in your life during this Lenten season? How can you remain attentive to God's leading moving forward?
- As we reflect on the end of the Israelites' journey in Exodus, what promises of God are you holding onto as you look ahead to the next chapter of your walk with God?

Grace and Peace,
Brother Ben